unlikely
TRUTHS
of
motherhood

unlikely TRUTHS *of* motherhood

Katie Van Dyke

CFI
Springville, Utah

© 2009 Katie Van Dyke

All rights reserved.

No part of this book may be reproduced in any form whatsoever, whether by graphic, visual, electronic, film, microfilm, tape recording, or any other means, without prior written permission of the publisher, except in the case of brief passages embodied in critical reviews and articles.

This is not an official publication of The Church of Jesus Christ of Latter-day Saints. The opinions and views expressed herein belong solely to the author and do not necessarily represent the opinions or views of Cedar Fort, Inc. Permission for the use of sources, graphics, and photos is also solely the responsibility of the author.

ISBN 13: 978-1-59955-289-7

Published by CFI, an imprint of Cedar Fort, Inc., 2373 W. 700 S., Springville, UT 84663
Distributed by Cedar Fort, Inc., www.cedarfort.com

LIBRARY OF CONGRESS CATALOGING-IN-PUBLICATION DATA

Van Dyke, Katie.
  Unlikely truths of motherhood / Katie Van Dyke.
    p. cm.
  ISBN 978-1-59955-289-7 (acid-free paper)
  1. Mothers--Religious life. 2. Motherhood--Religious aspects--Church of Jesus Christ of Latter-day Saints. 3. Motherhood--Religious aspects--Mormon Church. I. Title.

  BX8641.V33 2009
  248.8'431--dc22

2009009354

Cover design by Nicole Williams
Cover design © 2009 by Lyle Mortimer
Edited and typeset by Melissa J. Caldwell

Printed in the United States of America

10 9 8 7 6 5 4 3 2 1

Printed on acid-free paper

For my husband, Blair
And for our children, Christian, Caleb, Jeremiah, Ariel,
Seth, Micah, & Bethany
I'm so grateful our stories are all intertwined.

And for Lillian,
who illumines my story with her gift of color and light.

Other Books by Katie Van Dyke

Stop Struggling, Start Teaching
Stop Struggling, Start Parenting

Contents

Acknowledgments

ix

Sweet Monotony of Motherhood

1

The Indulgent Denial of Motherhood

25

The Exhilarating Exhaustion of Motherhood

51

CONTENTS

The Normal Chaos of Motherhood
79

About the Author
101

Acknowledgments

Thank you to Lyle Mortimer and his creative team at Cedar Fort for taking my words and ideas and placing them into this beautiful, tangible book. Thanks to Heather for your adept work and correspondence, to Melissa for your skillful editing, and to Nicole for your innovative designs.

Much gratitude goes to all the women who have shared this journey of motherhood with me. Thank you for sharing your joys and sorrows, triumphs and worries, insights and ideas. Your friendship strengthens and renews me, and your example and love adds depth and meaning to mothering.

Thanks and love to Summer and Stacy who have been there from the beginning; to Becky, Jana, and Cherlynn who were there even before the beginning; to Lori, Susan, Beth, Vivian, and Kara who shared the joys of little children with me; to Shelly, Sandy, Jaime, Barbara, and Teresa whose supportive hands continue to steady me as we raise our families together; to new moms and new friends, Stephanie and Janet; and to Jen, my cousin and kindred spirit. Keep those phone calls coming!

Also, special thanks and love to Jackie: Runners Unite! To Janice, Jan, and Shauna: Write On! To Tian: Long live the Classics! To Shannon and Phyllis: Let's do breakfast! And to Kristine: $400 *can* buy happiness!

Deep appreciation to Mom, Arlene, Grandma May, Grandma Van

Acknowledgments

Orden, and Samp. Thank you for showing me the way and for nurturing me along. To Jill and Sarah, I'm so grateful that motherhood has deepened our bond as sisters. And to my wonderful sisters-in-law Kristi, Kim, Becca, Linda, Tracy, and Jill.

I am humbly indebted to S. Kent Brown, professor, scholar, and friend. Thank you for bringing the lives of Mary, the mother of Jesus, and Elisabeth, the mother of John, close to my heart.

Finally, and with deep respect, thank you to the leaders of The Church of Jesus Christ of Latter-day Saints who support and sustain women in the sacred role of mother.

1
Sweet Monotony of Motherhood

When my sixth child, Micah, was born, I felt prompted to write down and record very honestly and openly all the feelings and emotions that come from having a new baby. To do this, I decided that I wanted to strip away all the experience that having five babies previously had given me and experience these feelings and emotions as a brand new mother would. Here's a sampling:

A Whole New World

As I sit in the dark and the quiet of my hospital room caring for my baby, I can't help but feel that he and I belong to a different world than the one going by outside—the one I have just come from. Could it be that I've been mistaken about the idea of bringing a baby into this world? Could it be that for a time, my baby has brought me into his world? After my husband experienced the birthing process with me and witnessed the power and pain that is involved in bringing a baby into this world, he described birth as reaching beyond the veil and literally yanking the baby into mortality. Perhaps the world I have come from is a place where my baby is reluctant to be, and perhaps it is best for me not to bring him into it right away. Instead, I must step into his world in order to prepare him to enter mine, and he, in turn, will teach me about his.

Leaving my own world behind will probably be the hardest part of entering my baby's world, especially since I can still see what is happening in my world. As I see others going about life as usual, I may feel isolated and alone, and the uncertainty of when I will be able to return to my world may deepen that sense of isolation. But as I focus on my baby instead of on the world I left behind, as I become more in tune with my baby's needs and more confident in my ability to fulfill them, I begin to understand that my baby's world is bigger than I once supposed.

The vastness of eternity closes in upon us as we sit here in the dark and quiet of our hospital room. It draws near us and just as I am cradling my baby, I feel cradled in the arms of a Heavenly parent. Being enfolded in the arms of eternity reminds me that my baby and I are not alone, and this helps me understand that the most important thing in life is sleeping in my arms.

I Want to Go Home!

Could it be that I am already weary of this world that only a week ago I so anticipated? Is it possible that I am that weak? The thought makes me ashamed of myself. Shame—only one of the many emotions that seem to beat down upon me like waves on the shore. Frustration, inadequacy, fear, and loneliness also wash over me, force me down, only for me to recover and have them wash over me once more. "Go Home!" they shout. "Back to your world; back to normal." Normal, I fear, is something I will never know again.

Of course, there are times of calm. Times when I look into my sleeping baby's face and feel joy and gratitude and love beyond anything I've ever known. Times when a silent something reaches out from his little spirit to mine and whispers, "I need you." And in the moments of the most extreme calm, I realize that it is not my baby telling me that he needs me but my own spirit assuring me that I need him. It tells me that striving to overcome these fears and emotions will make me stronger and that this little baby who depends on me for absolutely everything is actually helping me grow. So I will stay, and I will try—not just for my baby's sake, but for mine.

In My Baby's Eyes

My baby and I locked gazes today. He had been fussing, and as soon as he looked into my eyes, his crying stopped immediately. I cooed and talked to him for a moment until I realized that by looking into his eyes I was seeing my own reflection. But my reflection through my baby's eyes *was not the me I know—through the spirit, I recognized it as the me I can become. As my baby gazed up at me, I understood that he does not see my shortcomings and insecurities. He sees someone who will love him unconditionally and care for him unrelentingly. He does not see the fear and fatigue in me. Rather, he sees someone who will learn and endure. My baby sees the person Christ sees, and locked in his gaze, I wanted to become that person. Not long ago, I saw a picture of a river reflecting the sky above it. Looking at the river was like looking into the heavens, with no beginning and no ending. The blue of my baby's eyes reminds me of that picture. Looking into them, I'm drawn closer to heaven. Looking into them, I'm drawn closer to the person a want to be. Isn't it me that is supposed to be teaching that to my baby? What a surprise to be instructed by one so young.*

As a mother of six children, I was surprised to be surprised. And as I recorded one surprising entry after another, I came to see this truth: while mother's have a profound effect on the lives of their children, it is just as true that children have a profound effect on the lives of their mothers. Relating to this truth, a career oriented mother confided, "I think I was usually there for my children when they need me, but I'm not sure I was there when I needed them."[1] Like myself, this mother has stumbled onto an often overlooked truth about motherhood: we need our children just as much as they need us. Because this is a truth that is often overlooked, we'll call it an "unlikely truth."

In this book, we will focus on four of these unlikely truths of motherhood. They are the Sweet Monotony of Motherhood, the Indulgent Denial of Motherhood, the Exhilarating Exhaustion of Motherhood, and the Normal Chaos of Motherhood. These unlikely truths will help us see the power that comes into our lives as mothers when we allow our children to teach and inspire us. As we focus on each one, we will find truth in President Monson's observations that "the laughter of children gladdens our hearts . . . the faith of children soothes our souls . . . and the love of children prompts our deeds."[2] To begin, consider another entry in my journal illustrating the candid emotions of a new mother:

Sweet Monotony

Feeding
FeedingBurping
FeedingBurpingChanging
FeedingBurpingChangingCooing
FeedingBurpingChangingCooingFussing
FeedingBurpingChangingCooingFussingRocking
FeedingBurpingChangingCooingFussingRockingSleeping
FeedingBurpingChangingCooingFussingRockingSleepingWaking
BurpingChangingCooingFussingRockingSleepingWaking
ChangingCooingFussingRockingSleepingWaking
CooingFussingRockingSleepingWaking
FussingRockingSleepingWaking
RockingSleepingWaking
SleepingWaking
Waking
Though the order may change,
The motions are the same.
Regardless of time,
Regardless of day,
My life
And the life of my baby's
Is made up of the same movements
Over and
Over and
Over again.
It is exhausting
For both of us.
I sometimes long for a change. . . Does he?
But then I remember that
Music is made
Using the same seven notes in variation.
And only twenty-six letters combine
to create poems, and plays, and masterpieces.
I realize that monotony can create miracles.

> So I will go through the motions with my baby
> And we will dance
> Through the pages
> of our own story.

As a mother, I was strengthened and uplifted by this impression that the moments of motherhood that may seem the most monotonous accumulate to accomplish what is most rewarding and sweet for mothers. Motherhood is indeed hard work made up of tasks that seem never ending, repetitive, and seemingly dull. That, of course, is the monotony part of it all. However, calling motherhood monotonous without calling it sweet as well is like calling the night sky black without noticing the stars. To illustrate this point more poignantly, let me share an experience with you wherein I did not respect the rigors required of new mothers. Ironically, the experience was with the birth of my seventh child, after I'd been inspired by the sweet monotony of my sixth. Yet another indication that repetition is one of Heavenly Father's most powerful tools.

When my seventh baby was born, I was tired. We weren't going to have a seventh baby. With our numbers at five boys and one girl (any mother of boys knows that five of them is a lot!), we were ready to be done. But our only daughter, Ariel, who was six at the time, asked if she could pray for a baby sister. I told her she could but only after explaining that some prayers are answered in different ways than we expect and that maybe the sister she prayed for would come in the form of her own daughter some day or even a best friend sister-in-law. Ariel was undaunted by this explanation and began to pray each night for a baby sister. After more than a year of prayers without missing a single night, my heart and the heart of my husband were softened. We talked together and said, "You know, there are only two things standing in the way of Heavenly Father answering her prayers . . . you and me." We decided to exercise the same faith as our daughter, and through that faith, our family has been blessed with not just one but two little girls. Ariel was named after the city of Jerusalem (see Isaiah 29). And Bethany was named after the village of Bethany that borders Jerusalem where Jesus loved to spend time with his dear friends. Bethany's middle name is Faith to connect her to and remind her of the faith of her older sister.

Now that is an inspiring story! Yet, even so, when Bethany was born, I was tired! She was a docile baby and willing to be set aside, so set her aside I did. I did not respect the rhythms required to help a new baby thrive. As a result, she did not thrive. In fact, she shrunk and shriveled right before my eyes. The first time I even noticed it was the day before her two week checkup. Her new baby hospital pictures came in the mail. When I took them out to look at them, I gasped at the difference between the chubby and plump baby in the picture and my gaunt and drawn little daughter. Sure enough, at the doctor's the next day, I found that she had lost over a pound in her first two weeks of life.

The nurses were horrified. The doctor was concerned. They labeled her as failure to thrive. They pushed samples of formula into my arms and ordered me to supplement my breast feeding efforts. But I knew differently. I knew that her failure to thrive was due to my failure to strive. Now understand me. I know that there are many babies who fail to thrive without any fault on the mother's part. But this was not the case here. I had not respected the motions a mother must go through to raise a happy, healthy baby.

I took her home with a resolve to be the mother I knew I could be, relying on Heavenly Father's help to strengthen me. After all he has promised,

> Hast thou not known? Hast thou not heard, that the everlasting God, the Lord, the Creator of the ends of the earth, fainteth not, neither is weary. There is no searching of his understanding. He giveth power to the faint. And to them that have no might he increaseth their strength. . . . But they that wait upon the Lord shall renew their strength; they shall mount up with the wings as eagles; they shall run and not be weary; and they shall walk, and not faint. (Isaiah 40:28–29, 31).

After another month went by where I relied on this promise from Heavenly Father and fully entered into the Sweet Monotony of Motherhood, I wrote this:

Ah-h-h-h-h Bethany! She is growing and spitting up and pooping like crazy! Doing all the things a baby ought to do—smelling the way a baby ought to smell. I am so wholly connected to her through our labors and these smells, because they are such a part of me as well. Her head has that new baby musky smell, and I drink it in and love her so ferociously. It is interesting how interconnected everything is. There was a time when I didn't feel as connected to her as I do now. In fact, there was a time when I felt completely disconnected—when she wasn't growing, wasn't spitting, when her poop didn't smell just right. I brushed the feeling of emotional disconnect aside and chalked it up to fatigue and hormones, but now I see that it was more than that. It's hard to explain but by her not nursing well and as a result not spitting or pooping or having that sweet new baby breath and musky smell, she was somehow rejecting me, and I responded by disconnecting to her. Perhaps that's why mothers in the wild reject babies sometimes—the intricate dance of instincts is interrupted. But thank goodness the higher human mind continues working and doing and thinking to restore the balance and to have the dance ensue one more. She is more fussy now than she used to be but the bouncing and the rocking are part of the dance—a necessary step in her getting what she needs nutritionally and having it upset her a touch. So I will bounce and rock and smell and squeeze and enjoy this dance that will ultimately be over too soon.

And that's what sweet monotony is all about. It's how the striving brings the thriving. It's the law of the harvest. And what is true for every other act of labor is true for motherhood as well. We will reap what we sow. And Heavenly Father will help us, so even when we are bone weary tired, as mothers often are, if we believe that our strength can be renewed, if we believe that we can indeed mount on the wings of eagles, we will be magnified in the tasks we perform, and the results of our efforts will be magnified in such a way that we will see miracles. So as we continue to discuss the Sweet Monotony of Motherhood, we'll focus on the striving as well as the thriving. The striving essentially comprises all the work we as mothers are required to do. While the thriving is made up of all the miracles we see from our efforts, both in the lives of our children and in our own lives as well.

The Striving

The list is too long, our space limited, to talk about all the tasks that mothers perform for their children. There's the laundry, the cooking, the cleaning, the mending, the driving from here to there, the bandaging of wounds, the wiping up of spills, the dressing, the grooming, the soothing, the reading, the checking of homework, the signing of notes, and that's just a small dent in the seemingly endless list of tasks. In fact, in a recent *MSN Money* report, the price of a mom was placed at $138,095.[3] This figure was calculated by taking the wages that would have been paid to a stay-at-home mom in 2007 if she were paid for all the elements of her job. These elements included the following ten jobs that moms do on an average day: housekeeper, daycare center teacher, cook, computer operator, laundry machine operator, janitor, facilities manager, van driver, CEO, and psychologist. I would add to this list personal coach and life skills trainer since all the things moms do need to be taught to their children before their eighteenth birthday! It is exhausting and daunting.

I remember a Relief Society lesson given by a good friend of mine, who is also the mother of a large family. Most mothers of large families are highly esteemed, and this friend is no exception. She made all the Relief Society sisters feel better when she admitted that sometimes there were days when she just didn't want to get up in the morning and do it all again. But she went on to say that the reason she does it morning in and morning out is because she knows that it is what Heavenly Father wants her to do. She *believes* that through her efforts, her children will grow; yes, physically, but the miracle behind all the physical exertion is that our children grow in so many more ways than just physically. Listen to the way my good friend Jan Robinson puts it in her poem, "Mother's Homemade Bread."

Mother's Homemade Bread

When I think of Homemade bread,
The very thought just warms my heart.
My mind wanders back to returning home,
From long days at school . . .

And opening the back door off mother's kitchen
As the smell of freshly baked dough
would welcome us home.

It wasn't only the smell that would warm our hearts . . .
But the very thought that
Mom was home waiting for us to walk in the door,
To greet us and inquire about our day.
Somehow just knowing she was home with her apron on . . .
Mixing and stirring . . .
Molding and shaping . . .
Not only the bread to fill our empty stomachs,
But her smile and hugs to fill our sometimes empty souls.

Also, the fact that she was showing us that she had thought about
    us,
With fondness during her day . . .
Enough to get out her flour and mixing bowl
And cook up something to please our yearning taste buds.
Little did she know then . . .
That her small yet GIGANTIC act of Love,
Would Shape and mold us to become
Secure and productive human beings.

You see . . . Homemade Bread
Was more than just dough . . .
For us . . . it was LOVE

    Yes, making homemade bread is more than just an act of feeding our families. It is an act of love. And all the other physical exertions that we make in behalf of our children go beyond simply clothing or soothing or chauffeuring them, they are opportunities to teach, to connect, and to love. So while there is not time to go into all the physical tasks of motherhood, let's look at one of the most repetitive tasks there is: cooking.
    Shirley Klein, an associate professor in the School of Family Life at

Brigham Young University, said this about mealtime in an April 2005 BYU Devotional address:

> In our modern technological age, everything we do seems to be accelerated. It is easy for us individually to graze in our kitchens, dine from our dashboards, or to go to the nearest restaurant for a quick meal rather than go to the trouble of preparing a meal and sitting down together.
>
> Besides providing good food, family meals have numerous beneficial effects. Evidence suggests that family meals with parents present contribute to better nutritive intake, fewer psychological problems, and less risky or self-destructive behavior. Family meals also play an important role in preventing unhealthy weight-control practices.
>
> Along with the physical benefit of family meals, the simple domestic act of creating a meal and enjoying it together is an important connector for families. The meal doesn't have to be elaborate to create a time to connect and get a feeling for each person's day. At home, outside distractions can be managed so emphasis is on interaction. The regular, expected mealtime experience gives children a sense of security. These simple, everyday routines have great power in our lives.[4]

Now I have a confession to make about meal preparation. In our home, my husband does all of the cooking. Most women are pretty jealous when they hear that. In my own defense, let me tell you what it took to get my husband, who is a far better cook than me, to take over the cooking. First, you have to have five children in seven and a half years. And then that fifth child has got to be so fussy and have too many ear infections to count and you have to have not slept in ten months so that sleep deprivation and emotional distress has brought you and your husband to the understanding that you are a self-proclaimed nut case. At that point, your husband will probably pick up the slack somewhere, and in my case, it was cooking. (I think it also had something to do with the fact that he was tired of eating Taco Bell every night and was starting to put on weight because of the cinnamon twists).

But despite the fact that I do not cook, and therefore, do not nurture my children with food, Heavenly Father provided me with a poignant experience of the power that can come into your life when you are fed and nurtured at a table by someone who loves you. For me, that someone is a wonderful woman in our ward named Lillian Rittmanic.

I was assigned to visit teach Lillian, and at the time, she was approaching eighty years of age. I already knew and loved Lillian. She is one of those women who is full of genuine charity for others. You always get a glimpse of who you really are when you are with her, because she has a talent for seeing others the way Christ sees them. She is an amazing artist. For our discussion, it's important to add that she put away her paint brushes when she was raising her family. She said her children were the most important portraits she could create, so she did not start painting again until her children were fully raised. But while I was excited to visit teach Lillian, I was worried how my little children would do in a home not conducive, at the time, for little children. My fears were unfounded, however, because she welcomed us into her home with enthusiasm. In fact, she welcomed us into her home each time with lunch! Generally it was just frozen pizza and fruit and drinks. But it was always served on a nice table cloth with nice plates and cups and genuine love. And this all happened at a time when I was in particular need of nurturing.

I was pregnant with my seventh baby at the time, and I was very sick. I had never been sick with a pregnancy before so this was new to me. The same hormones that were making me sick were also making me a little depressed, and then once my baby was born, I continued to get bacterial infections of one kind or another for the first three months. So after one entire year of illness, I was worn down in every way imaginable: physically, mentally, spiritually, emotionally, and so on. But once a month, I would walk into Lillian's home and through her small meal and nurturing, I would be lifted. I felt loved. I felt secure. As Shirley Klien stated, this simple routine had great power in my life.

In section 98 of the Doctrine and Covenants we read, "For he will give unto the faithful line upon line, precept upon precept; and I will try you and prove you herewith" (D&C 98:12). If we prove faithful in the little things, the bigger things will be added upon. As far as cooking is concerned, we provide the meal and Heavenly Father will provide the miracle! This is true for all of our family duties. Again, from

Shirley Klein, speaking of all family duties:

> These activities have purpose and must not be disregarded or interfered with. In the settings of everyday work and recreation, families can learn about moral truths, make choices, and practice honesty, patience, brotherly kindness and charity. Everyday home events can seem so simple that we may overlook them, but because they are simple, frequent, and repeated, they offer valuable opportunities to build individuals and families. . . . In our everyday home activities, we learn lessons of life that build strong character. The integrative nature of everyday living provides opportunities to gain strength in many ways—physically, intellectually, socially, and spiritually. . . We should remember that daily activities of the home like feeding and clothing ourselves has the power to help us practice obedience, service, love, and cooperation.[5]

So while our list of monotonous tasks seems never ending, Professor Klein also provides an impressive array of words to describe the miracles the monotony creates: deeper understanding of moral truth, improved ability to make good choices, honesty, patience, brotherly kindness, and charity, opportunities to build strong character, gain strength, and grow physically, intellectually, socially, and spiritually, power to practice obedience, service, love, and cooperation. All of these things are definitely the "bigger things added on" as we "prove faithful in the little things."

I think it's interesting to note here the difference between the promises of the Lord and the promises of the world regarding motherhood. The Lord promises us that if we do what we can, He will magnify us. We do the little things. He provides the big things. It's a promise. A covenant given to us by our most loyal and loving Brother. The world, on the other hand, tells us that we have to do the big things and then promises us nothing. It's worse than that, in fact, because not only does the world promise us nothing, it threatens us with loss if we don't do things in a worldly way: "If we do not seek a career, we will never know who we are," "if we choose to stay at home, we are wasting our talents," or "we will never be able to give anything to anybody else if we do not fulfill our own needs first." The lures of the world are strong in their attempts to pull mothers out of their homes, but we must remember that those lures are lies.

My dear friend Lillian was away from home on her eightieth birthday, so I sent her a card in the mail. In return, I received this beautiful reply that illustrates that in her wisdom, she is not deceived by the lies of the world.

> Whenever I think of you, Katie, and you pop into my thoughts and prayers often, I picture you that Sunday after Relief Society was over—holding your baby, and one by one, your children and your husband gathered around you. What a lovely sight! Do you have any idea how many "corporate woman" after they have received their "proverbial gold watch" upon retirement — how much they would give to turn back the clock and trade places with you!!! When your children are grown, I'm sure that your children will continue to gather around you and garnish your life in ways that you can't even imagine. After years of involvement with fevers, runny noses, diapers—all night sleepless sessions with sick, many sick, babies—challenges that seemed to have no solutions—all of a sudden one day they are looking lovingly into your eyes and saying, "Bye, mom, I'm off to college," or wherever "See you later." And the stunning thought occurs, "It's over and I'm not done with them. I want them back. There's still things to do." And you say good-bye because you know that's the way it's supposed to be. They must leave the nest called home and continue on the learning journey. Then, Katie, you will have the wonderful gift in place that you can ever give yourself—and that is peace of mind—knowing that every minute those wonderful children were nurtured by you—you did the best you could—even though most of the time you were "cross eyed weary." It's worth it, Katie! I speak from experience. It's worth it!

Lillian is a very wise woman, combating the lies of the world with truth and testimony. Read the words President Gordon B. Hinckley uses to combat the lies of the world:

> It is so tremendously important that the women of the Church stand strong and immovable for that which is correct and proper under the plan of the Lord. We call upon the women of the church to stand together for righteousness. They must begin in their homes. . . . They must be the teachers and the guardians of their daughters. . . . When you save a girl, you save generations. I see this as the one bright shining hope in a world that is marching toward self-destruction. . . . We must never lose sight of the strength of women. It is mothers who set

the tone of the home. It is mothers who most directly affect the lives of their children. It is mothers who teach infants to pray, who read to them choice and beautiful literature from the scriptures and other sources. It is mothers who nurture them and bring them up in the ways of the Lord. Their influence is paramount. President Heber J. Grant said, "Without the devotion and absolute testimony of the living God in the hearts of our mothers this Church would die."[6]

I think this is an amazing statement. It says that motherhood is amazing. It says that motherhood is powerful. It essentially says that the Sweet Monotony of Motherhood creates miracles. It says that incredible striving brings amazing thriving. So let's look at the thriving. First, as it relates to our children and then as it relates to us.

The Thriving: Our Children

We have already touched upon many of the wonderful things that can happen in our family's lives as we strive to serve them. But many of these things are hard to measure. Unlike the more exact science of cooking where carefully following a recipe brings expected results (except in my case, that is), the results of a mother's striving are less measurable and sometimes hard to see. But I do have a couple of measures that help me to know I am going in the right direction with my children. When these two measures are in place, it is easier for me to have faith and trust in Heavenly Father that miracles are forthcoming. The measures are laughter and the enjoyment that comes from spending time with my children. Let's look at laughter first.

I knew I needed to work on my ability to laugh with my children when my son Jeremy brought the lack of laughter in my life to my attention. He was twelve at the time, and my husband was leading a tour group in Israel with our oldest son Christian, so I was going it alone with our six other children. My husband, institute teacher though he is, is also a Harley Davidson enthusiast. One of the highlights of his life came when he was finally able to buy a Harley Davidson of his own. The acquisition of this motorcycle, in fact, is so important that we celebrate its birthday each year—just like it was one of the children. But for the Harley's fourth birthday, my husband left on his Israel tour, so he left strict instructions to celebrate the Harley's birthday without him. The traditional celebration is baking the Harley a cake, covering it with foil, poking candles through the foil, then while holding it up to the Harley's exhaust pipe and singing "Happy Birthday to You," we start the Harley and the exhaust "blows" out the candles.

Everything went according to plan until it was time to roll the Harley out into the driveway. Not being a Harley enthusiast myself, I had no idea how heavy the bike was. I envisioned myself putting up the kick stand and simply rolling it out of the garage. Much to my dismay, when I put up the kick stand, the bike nearly fell over and crushed me. It was all I could do to get it back up right. Undaunted, I called to Jeremy, twelve, and Caleb, fourteen, to help me. Even with the three of us, it was still an almost impossible project, but we managed somehow, despite the fact that we were laughing all the while. We could just imagine how horrified my husband would be if he could see what was happening to his precious Harley, and with tears of laughter streaming down our cheeks and beads of sweat dripping off our foreheads, Jeremy looked at me in amazement and said, "Mom, I've never seen you laugh like this before." I was sobered by his statement, because I believe that laughter is a gift. Yet as a mother, I had neglected to give my children the gift of laughter. I determined then and there to laugh more with my children.

This is what Sister Marjorie Pay Hinckley says about laughing, "The only way to get through life is to laugh your way through it. You either have to laugh or cry. I prefer to laugh. Crying gives me a headache."[7]

This gift of laughter that Sister Hinckley possesses is a natural quality inherent within children. The BYU school of Family Life published an article by Gary K. Palmer reporting that children laugh four hundred times a day while adults laugh fifteen! Wow! Now, before you think this means children are too lightminded, consider that this article also reports: that "[laughter] is the way we see things; it's the way we think; it's an attitude, not an event. Perhaps the key lies in becoming more childlike."[8]

We've been told many times to become like a little child, and this article offers one reason why. It asserts that "laughter is more important than a family vacation, because it's always available, it can happen every day, and it's free. Happy families are those living together every day and making the most of it. Laughter is like getting away without going away. It gives you a break."[9] As found in Proverbs 17:22, "A merry heart doeth good like a medicine."

Palmer continues, "Laughter improves communication and builds relationships because everyone laughs in the same language. Your children will remember your humor much longer than they will the things you buy them. Children are more receptive when they are having fun. Laughter helps us remember. Humor creates an unforgettable learning experience because it makes us laugh and feel good . . . [it] builds friendships, [and] families that laugh together are inseparable."[10]

Here's a funny story from a talk entitled "Now That's Funny" by Joni Hilton. It illustrates this point that laughter is both memorable and unifying. She writes, "We have a son who is very innovative and a good problem solver. One night we went out to dinner, and he had ordered french fries; for some reason, his order came before anyone else's. You know how that is: you are sitting there, smelling these salty, greasy, wonderful fries. So one by one, we were reaching over and stealing some of his french fries. He looked around at this situation, sized up what he had to do, and spit on his french fries. He had them all to himself."[11]

Of this, and other experiences, Joni Hilton declares, "There are so many situations for Mormon women to laugh in, I can't believe it. It's a miracle we ever stop laughing, because life around us is hilarious. When you have children, as we Mormon women tend to do, you have laughter. They are linked traits—they just seem to go together."[12]

So soak up your children's laughter, and use this as a measure for the Sweet Monotony of Motherhood. As you do this, you will find that laughter is inseparably linked to the second measure, which is enjoying the time you spend with your children.

To introduce the measure of enjoying the time you and your children spend together, let's turn to King David of the Old Testament. The story of King David and Bath-sheba is a familiar one. In the "eveningtide . . . [David] walked upon the roof of [his] house . . . he saw a woman washing herself; and the woman was very beautiful to look upon . . . David sent messengers, and took her; and she came in unto him, and he lay with her . . . and the woman conceived, and sent and told David, and said, I am with child (see 2 Samuel 11:2-5).

When David learned that Bath-sheba was pregnant, he went to great lengths to cover up this sin of adultery. He sent for Bath-sheba's husband, Uriah the Hittite, with the intent to send him to his home so he would lie with Bath-sheba. But Uriah didn't return to his home. Instead, he slept with the king's servants outside of David's Palace gates. When David inquired why Uriah had not returned home to Bathsheba, Uriah replied, "The ark, and Israel, and Judah, abide in tents; and my lord Joab, and the servants of my lord, are encamped in the open fields; shall I then go into mine house, to eat and to drink, and to lie with my wife? As thou livest, and as thy soul liveth, I will not do this thing" (2 Samuel 11:11).

David then attempted to get Uriah drunk in order that he might return to his home, but when this also failed, David wrote a letter to Joab saying, "Set ye Uriah in the forefront of the hottest battle, and retire ye from him, that he may be smitten and die. . . and Joab . . . assigned Uriah unto a place where he knew that valiant men were . . . and there fell some of the servants of David; and Uriah the Hittite died also" (2 Samuel 11:14–17)

The story of King David's transgressions is one of the most lamentable in all scripture. But you may be asking, "What does this have to do with our discussion on motherhood?" The key lies in verse 1 of 2 Samuel 11. We often think that David's initial sin is lusting after Bathsheba, but that is not true. Verse one, reveals David's first mistake: "And it came to pass, after the year was expired, at the time when kings go forth to battle, that David sent Joab, and his servants with him, and all Israel; and they destroyed the children of Ammon, and besieged Rabbah, but David tarried still at Jerusalem."

King David "tarried." He wasn't where a king needed to be. Had David been where he was supposed to be, this set of tragic circumstances would not have taken place. As mothers, we need to be where our children are. President Harold B. Lee taught, "Keep the mother of your home at the 'crossroads' of the home. There is a great danger today of homes breaking down because of allurements to entice mothers to neglect their being at home as family members are coming to or going from the home."[13]

President Ezra Taft Benson echoed this admonition when he spoke to mothers saying, "Be at the crossroads when your children are coming or going—when they leave and return from dates, when they bring friends home. Be there at the crossroads whether they are 6 or 16. In Proverbs we read, 'A child left to himself bringeth his mother to shame' (Proverbs 29:15). Among the greatest concerns in our society are the millions of latchkey children who come home daily to empty houses, unsupervised by working parents."[14]

King David's choices led to eternal negative consequences. Our choices as mothers will also have eternal consequences. Let us not "tarry" elsewhere, but be where mothers ought to be—with our children.

Once, while preparing a presentation I was giving on motherhood, my eight-year-old son Seth asked me what I was doing. I told him that I was getting ready to teach others about how important it is to be a mother. He looked a bit confused for a moment and then asked this question, "How can you teach other people when you never leave the house?" While a little taken back by this question, I found that it brought me a feeling of pleasant satisfaction. In my children's eyes, I am where I am supposed to be.

I love this insight from Catherine Newman:

> Modern life might tend to encourage the secular version of a pie-in-the-sky mentality—you'll be happier, it promises, on the weekend or in a bigger house or at the mall or after you retire—but what [we] are advocating is heaven on earth. When we become aware of this, "might it not suggest how precious time we do share together with our children is, and how to hold our essentially fleeting moments with them in awareness? Might it not influence how we hug and kiss our children, and say good-night to them, and watch them sleep, and wake them in the morning?"
>
> Last night I lay in bed with my children as they were falling asleep, and I stopped making lists in my head. I stopped fretting . . . I stopped wishing the kids would fall asleep already so I could be somewhere else, doing something else.
>
> Instead, I noticed the dark crescents of their eyelashes. I watched as the moonlight turned their cheeks to white apricots. And I felt my heart swell with joy and gratitude. It was utterly ordinary. And it was utterly extraordinary. It was an every day blessing.[15]

I recently had one of these utterly ordinary yet utterly extraordinary everyday blessings by spending time with my children. In front of our house during the summer, a steady stream of water runs in our gutter. This water comes from a few houses up the road from us who do not water their lawns with sprinkler systems, but who irrigate their lawns with what is known as "water rights." Now, I'm a city girl, and this way of watering lawns was new to me. It was also new to me to find out that it wasn't culinary water they were using and, therefore, the water running down my gutter wasn't safe to drink—EW! But as you all know, wherever there is water, there is also children playing in the water, and my children were no exception. But being a city girl, I wasn't thrilled about having my kids play in "unsanitary" water. I tried to discourage it, but it was like trying to keep bees away from honey, so play they did. They would often ask if I would play in the water with them, but I thought that one of us needed to stay healthy if we were to catch some water born epidemic. So for years—eight years to be exact—my children played in the water in front of our house while I refused to even dip my big toe in it.

All that changed during the summer of 2006. That summer, I was asked to speak to a group of mothers about the importance of spending time with their children. To prepare for the talk, I read story after story about mothers enjoying children immensely and about the pleasure brought to them when they just soaked their children up. So that summer, I soaked my own children up! One of the ways I did that was to take the plunge of wading into the water in front of our house for the first time. It was great! We had a blast. We splashed and splattered and laughed and screamed, and while I was careful not to get my wet hands near my mouth or my eyes, I thoroughly enjoyed the time I spent with my children. In fact, I enjoyed it so much that even after my children had tired of the water and were playing other things in the yard, I continued to wade in the gutter with the water running over my feet.

I could not get enough of the sound of the water lapping against my feet and then gurgling past me. And as I listened to the sound of running water, I couldn't help but think that we must all be instinctively connected to that sound. Long before pipes were invented to carry water directly into homes, people needed to settle near running water in order to survive physically. This thought led me to think about our spiritual needs for living water and that we must all be intimately connected to Christ, the Living Water, for spiritual survival purposes. My thoughts turned to those who have been raised by goodly parents and taught about the truths of the gospel, but for one reason or another have chosen other paths at this time in their lives. I thought how these people must be thirsty for the Living Water they are missing in their lives. But I was comforted to know that their spiritual thirst will not be quenched until they come back to Christ. And I knew there and then, standing in the gutter in front of my home with the sound of water gurgling at my feet, that their search would bring them back to Christ—that they would seek the Living Water to keep their spiritual selves alive.

The point that I am making with this experience is that I love nothing more than to think deep thoughts. And I thought these deep thoughts while playing with my children. And these thoughts were connected and amplified in feeling and meaning by the presence of the Spirit, because where our children are, the Spirit is thick: thick with love, thick with learning, thick with joy, thick with understanding. So while getting *way* into the lives of my children, I was blessed with the things I most love and most need as well. It reminded me of something I had written a long time ago,

> Have your dreams while you do your duty,
> and soon your duty will become your dreams.
> Because Heavenly Father would never ask us to do anything
> that does not ultimately bring us joy and satisfaction.

Dorothy in *The Wizard of Oz* learns the same thing from her amazing journey. She says, "If I ever go looking for my heart's desire again, I won't look any further than my own backyard. Because if it isn't there, I never really lost it to begin with."

The Scarecrow declares of this lesson, "But that's so easy! I should have thought of it for you." The Tin Man adds, "I should have felt it in my heart." As Mormon mothers, we know both in our minds and in our hearts that "there's no place like home!"

President Spencer W. Kimball agrees. He writes, "Bear in mind, dear sisters, that the eternal blessings which are yours through membership in The Church of Jesus Christ of Latter-day Saints are far, far greater than any other blessings you could possibly receive. No greater recognition can come to you in this world than to be known as a woman of God. No greater status can be conferred upon you than being a daughter of God who experiences true sisterhood, wifehood, and motherhood."[16]

So here we have the evidence that our striving not only helps our children thrive, but it also enables us to *thrive* in the ways that are most important and most lasting. As we share our children's lives with them, as we become fully immersed in the work of motherhood, we can become witnesses of miracles not only in their growth and development, but in ours as well.

The Thriving: Mothers

Trisa Martin recounts how she learned that striving for our children brings thriving for us as mothers. She writes:

> "What a disaster!" I exclaimed staring at the toys, books, and clothes scattered helter-skelter throughout the house by my three children. I could hear the baby crying in his room down the hall. Could he be awake already? Walking wearily to his room, I could smell from the door the reason he woke up crying. Diapers and disasters, I thought. So this was motherhood.
>
> Hearing the doorbell chime, I hurried to the door, only to find that no one was there. Instead, a tattered basket sat on the doorstep, stuffed with daffodils, a praying mantis egg sac, rocks, bunches of fresh grass, and a folded piece of paper. "To Mom," read the blue crayon scrawl. "We love you."
>
> I lingered a moment, halted by emotion and questions. I had chosen to leave behind a satisfying teaching career to become a homemaker, but now I wondered, was I becoming a joyful mother of children or a martyr? Did I consider my children a blessing or a burden? Gazing at my children's basket that spring morning, I realized that in fact I was in a classroom of sorts. But this time my children were teaching me. Our course of study? Becoming like the Savior.
>
> The lesson of the daffodils and praying mantis eggs was reinforced

late one evening as I was busy finishing my remaining tasks. "Come see the sunset, Mom," my daughter begged, rushing into the kitchen. In annoyance, I started to say, "I can't, I'm too . . . ," but she grabbed my hand and pulled me outside to see a brilliant sky exploding with crimson and gold.

"Sunsets don't wait," she said.

While learning the ABCs, my children teach me laughter and joy. Digging up newly planted bushes or assembling a band to serenade our neighbors, my children teach me patience. Through daily, affectionate hugs, they teach me love. Along with diapers, messes, daffodils, praying mantis eggs, rocks, sunsets, and scrawled love notes, my children daily give me gifts of love and insight that tutor me toward becoming more like Jesus Christ and Heavenly Father.[17]

This account provides the sweetest truth about the Sweet Monotony of Motherhood, and that is that as we fulfill this important task, we are becoming more and more like our Savior. As mothers, we are not here to bide our time until our children grow up and we can do something else. *Being* a mother is *becoming* who Heavenly Father wants us to be. I was taught this poignant principle during a routine trip to the doctor's office.

Journal Entry: Jan. 17, 2006

As Seth, Micah, Bethany, and I walked across the parking lot towards the Dr.'s office, the sun cast our shadows on the pavement. I had Bethany on my left hip and used my right hand to hold Micah's hand. Seth was also connected to us by holding Micah's left hand. This intimate connection of the four of us, cast in shadow, was a revelation to me of who I really am. As I observed it, I thought, "That's me. I am made up of what I see there. My shadow alone would be incomplete. I would not be whole. Without my kids, I would be missing appendages or parts absolutely necessary for defining who I am." It was an immensely satisfying thought—a thought filled with TRUTH—a TRUTH so big and wonderful that mere words do not even begin to do it justice. But to attempt it, the thought becomes ever grander when I consider the work and the glory of Heavenly Father, which is to bring to pass the immortality and eternal life of man. He wants me to become one with Him—to become a part of Him just as my children are apart of me. So that when his Shadow is cast, I am there on His right hand with

> Bethany on my hip, holding Micah's hand, who is holding Seth's hand, who is holding Ariel's and Jeremy's and Caleb's and Christian's—and there will be children's spouses and grandchildren, all of us having become one with Him through Christ. As I said, words don't quite give the thought justice but hopefully they can at least capture a glimpse of TRUTH.

And the "glimpse of truth" captured by the Sweet Monotony of Motherhood is that we, as mothers, are one of the fruits of our efforts. Consider that! We always look to our children as the greatest fruits of motherhood. We look to the eternal blessing of forever families as a much desired fruit. And of course, these fruits are exceedingly desirable. But becoming who Heavenly Father wants us to be and filling the measure of our own creation, is a fruit that is just as desirable.

Motherhood is filled with so many important truths. The Sweet Monotony of Motherhood is just a portion of the truths we will find as we embrace this noble work. I believe that when the entirety of the truth about motherhood is known and understood that it will fill our hearts to the point of bursting because it will be so powerful. If, as you have read, you have felt a swelling of knowledge and understanding in your heart, I believe that you have been touched by a portion of truth. But remember, it is just a portion, and more of the truth about motherhood must be sought. The thirteenth article of faith reminds us to seek after, "anything virtuous, lovely, of good report or praiseworthy." Motherhood is most definitely virtuous, lovely, of good report, and praiseworthy, so it must be sought after. And the truths of motherhood must be sought after again and again since the adversary will attempt to block our efforts and persuade us to believe as the world believes. Remember that the reason this persuasion in so strong is because motherhood is so powerful. As Harold B. Lee said, "If you would reform the world from error and vice, begin by enlisting the mothers. The future of society is in the hands of mothers. If the world were in danger, only the mothers could save it."[18] So tirelessly seek to understand the truths about motherhood. In the remainder of this book, we will consider three other unlikely truths about motherhood, but they are not comprehensive. There will always be more knowledge to learn. There will always be more understanding to find. There will always be more wisdom to gain—especially with regards to motherhood.

Notes

1. Linda Eyre, *A Joyful Mother of Children* (Salt Lake City: ShadowMountain, 2002), 12.
2. Thomas S. Monson, "Precious Children, a Gift from God," *Ensign,* June 2000, 2–5.
3. MSN Money Staff, "The Price of a Mom, $138,095," MSN, http://.moneycentral.msn.com/CollegeAndFamily/ RaiseKids/ThePriceOfAMom.
4. Shirley Klein, "Preserving the Sacred Home," *BYU Magazine*, Summer 2005, 56–57.
5. Ibid., 57.
6. Gordon B. Hinckley, Worldwide Leadership Training, Jan. 2004.
7. Marjorie Pay Hinckley, *Glimpses* (Salt Lake City: Deseret Book, 1999), 107.
8. Gary K. Palmer, "Laughter, the Perfect Family Medicine," *Marriage & Families,* Summer 2005, 23.
9. Ibid.
10. Ibid.
11. Joni Hilton, "Now That's Funny," *To Mother, With Love* (American Fork: Covenant Communications, 2006), 21–32.
12. Ibid.
13. "Chapter 15: The Righteous Influence of Mothers," *Teachings of the Presidents of the Church: Harold B. Lee* (Salt Lake City: The Church of Jesus Christ of Latter-day Saints, 2000), 279.
14. *The Sermons and Writings of Ezra Taft Benson* (Salt Lake City: The Church of Jesus Christ of Latter-day Saints, 2003), 218.
15. Catherine Newman, "Dalai Mama," *Wondertime,* Spring 2006, 93.
16. Spencer W. Kimball, "The Role of Righteous Women," *Ensign,* Nov. 1979, 102.
17. Trisa Martin, "A Little Child Shall Lead Them," *Ensign,* June 2005, 57.
18. Harold B. Lee, *The Teachings of Harold B. Lee* (Salt Lake City: Bookcraft, 1996), 290.

2
The Indulgent Denial of Motherhood

Having learned in the first chapter that I am a reluctant cook, to say the least, you may be surprised that in this chapter, I've armed myself with a recipe to share with you. Even the most novice of cooks tend to have something they can throw together, and I am no exception. Most of the meals that I throw together involve mixing three or four ingredients and nothing more. In fact, my motto with my recipes is, "If I can do it, anyone can do it." And that's the kind of recipe you'll read about here. But this recipe does not involve any food items. It involves three simple concepts that when mixed together provide a recipe for indulging mothers. At first glance, this recipe may seem like one of denial, but as you read it, keep in mind this quote from Elder Maxwell, "Ironically, the natural man, who is so very selfish in so many ordinary ways, is strangely unselfish in that he reaches for too few of the things that bring real joy. He settles for a mess of pottage instead of eternal joy."[1] So to the natural man, this recipe my seem like a mess of pottage, but with spiritual eyes, we can see it as one of decadence and indulgence.

Let me explain to you why I have in my possession a recipe for indulging mothers. It's because in my early years as a mother I experienced some rather unsuccessful Mother's Days. In fact, Mother's Day became a day that I did not look forward to. But before I go on, let me vindicate my husband and children. They tried to make my Mother's Days successful, but nothing they could do lived up to my idealized fantasy of what a Mother's Day should be. You know the one I mean: Breakfast in bed, a long soak in a tub full of rose petals, the perfect present, time enough to do all the reading and napping I want while my children behave like perfect angels, and my husband tends to my every need without even having to be told what those needs are. I have a friend who told me that expectations are a reservation for resentment. And believe me, I made reservations each Mother's Day at the Resentment Hotel. What husband or children could live up to the fantasy I had created? Fortunately, I realized that none could. I realized that they were doing their best and that I was the misguided one. So I set out to determine what I could do to make Mother's Day successful, and over the years, I have come up with this recipe that not only makes for a successful Mother's Day but is one mothers can indulge themselves in all year long.

Ingredient #1

The first ingredient in this recipe is *unselfishness*. Now before you roll your eyes and say, "Of course. A mother couldn't possibly be happy unless she were making some kind of sacrifice." Please bear with me and I think you will see that this recipe item is sweeter than it seems. Unselfishness became the first item in my recipe when I came across an article describing the origins of Mother's Day. I learned that early Mother's Day celebrations in the United States were actually days where mothers united to promote causes that mothers are most passionate about. Examples from the early 1900s include Julia Ward Howard (author of the lyrics to the "Battle Hymn of the Republic") organizing mothers to rally for peace since she believed they bore the loss of human life more harshly than anyone else. Also, Anna Jarvis, an Appalachian homemaker, organized mothers to raise awareness of poor health conditions in her community. When Anna Jarvis died, her daughter, also named Anna Jarvis, began a campaign to memorialize a day where she could honor her mother. As a young girl, she remembered her mother giving a Sunday School lesson where she said, "I hope and pray that someone, sometime, will found a memorial mother's day. There are many days for men, but none for mothers." From 1905 to 1914, nearly ten years, Anna worked tirelessly lobbying businessmen and writing letters to politicians until at last Woodrow Wilson signed a bill recognizing Mother's Day as a national holiday.[2]

This story both shamed and inspired me. When I considered that a woman with no children of her own and a mother who had already passed away would work so hard to honor her mother, I was ashamed that I had wasted so many Mother's Days thinking only of myself. But it also inspired me to spend Mother's Day being a better daughter and granddaughter, daughter-in-law, and friend. Now, on Mother's Day, I keep a prayer in my heart for my mom, my mother-in-law, my grandmothers, and all those women who are examples of motherhood to me. I supplicate Heavenly Father to bring to these women's memories the moments of motherhood that have brought them the most joy. And in doing so, it never fails that Heavenly Father, through the gift of the Holy Ghost, blesses me with memories too, and I find myself engulfed in thoughts of joyful moments with my mother, my grandmothers, my mother-in-law, and my own children.

But I would not try to convince you of the importance of unselfishness using only the example of Anna Jarvis's. My testimony of the importance of unselfishness grew stronger when I read Elder Neal A. Maxwell's talk "The Precious Promise." He taught that on the day of Christ's infinite suffering, "He still noticed and nurtured finite sufferers who endured much less anguish than He had to bear. For instance, He noticed and restored an assailant's severed ear in the Garden of Gethsemane. On the cross, He directed John to take care of His mother, Mary, and he comforted a thief on a nearby cross."[3] With this in mind, Elder Maxwell admonishes, "When you and I let ourselves get stuck in the ooze of our own self-pity, we fail to notice the needs of others. Still, with a little more effort, we can become a little more noticing and a little more nurturing."[4] If my Savior can be unselfish during the days that brought the eternities its greatest events, I can surely be unselfish on days when I am most tired, depressed, moody, or sick. On these days, if I can turn my attention away from myself and towards my children, my unselfishness can turn into a time of great blessings for me. Here is just such an example from a journal entry.

Wonderful Whimper

As I was rocking Bethany for her nap, it was evident that she wasn't feeling well. She whined and coughed and cried as I tried to soothe her. Finally, she began to settle down but every now and then she would let out a little whimper. I was so tired myself. Tears started to flow and I lifted my head to heaven and let out a whimper of my own. Like an echo, Bethany whimpered again, and as I turned my attention towards her to soothe her, I knew that Heavenly Father was there for me, too. And knowing this about my Heavenly Father's readiness, willingness, and immense desire to help me, I was strengthened in my resolve to help Bethany. Just as I needed Heavenly Father, she needed me, and just as Heavenly Father is always there for me, I will always be there for her. A circle of succoring buoyed me up by a power I can only begin to comprehend. As hard as this is on a moment to moment basis, I am privileged to play such a key role in the service of Heavenly Father's children. The scripture "When ye have done it unto the least of these my brethren, ye have done it unto me," is even more meaningful to me now. What wonderful wisdom a whimper can bring.

Ingredient #2

The second ingredient for a successful Mother's Day stems out of the knowledge that the original celebrations of Mother's Day were used to promote causes dear to the hearts of women. Did you know that as Anna Jarvis watched Mother's Day change from these kinds of activities to more gift-giving activities, she began to regret that she had ever started the Mother's Day tradition. She believed that the day's sentiment was being sacrificed at the expense of greed and profit.[5] Knowing this, I began to think that at Thanksgiving, we reflect upon our blessings. During Christmas, we reflect on how we can be more Christlike. New Year's brings resolutions, and on Valentine's Day we commit to being better sweethearts. On Mother's Day, then, why not reflect on how we can become better mothers? So *reflection* is the second ingredient in the recipe.

But before you proceed to add reflection to unselfishness, know that this ingredient comes with a warning. You can't use just any kind of reflection. Generic brands will not do, and please do not use the artificial form. If you do, you are setting yourself up for discouragement and frustration. Let me explain. On a Mother's Day not long ago, I was reflecting on ways to be a better mother. On that day, I had an experience where new ideas were coming into my mind at an alarmingly rapid pace. I remember walking upstairs to my bedroom, and with each step I took, a new thought would present itself: your house should be cleaner; your hair should be lighter; your children should work harder; your husband should be home more often; you should be healthier; you should be thinner; your baby should be weaned so you can get more done. . . . And on and on until when I at last reached my bedroom, the words in my mind were so weighty that I could barely stand up straight. Reflecting on improvement had not inspired me, it had made my burdens too heavy to bear. And then in a flash, I knew the source from whence those words had come. I stomped my foot and said aloud, "What kind of friend are you? What kind of friend would take weariness and weigh me down with it?" And I knew that it was no friend of mine at all, but my adversary. So then turning to the Spirit, to my true friend, I asked "Why am I so affected by his words?" The answer was instantaneous, "You don't trust me enough." Now this answer might sound like a chastisement, but I had just experienced what it felt like to listen to lies, and this simple statement "You don't trust me enough" filled me with light and truth. And almost as instantaneous as this came, I also saw a vison of myself—a me who was less susceptible to the lies of Satan because I had greater trust in Heavenly Father's truths. I knew that these latter reflections were the brand name kind of reflections. I knew that they had come from the Holy Ghost. Listen to how President James E. Faust expressed it, "The Comforter can be with us as we seek to improve. It can function as a source of revelation . . . and also help keep us from making mistakes. It can enhance our natural senses so that we can see more clearly, hear more keenly, and remember what we should remember. It is a way of maximizing our happiness."[6]

As we add reflections to our mixing bowl, then, remember that reflections for improvement from the Holy Ghost will bring us happiness even while pointing out mistakes. I don't need to lighten my hair or keep my house cleaner. I don't need to nag my husband to be home more or even to wean my baby. I simply need to trust my Heavenly Father more. And as my experience illustrates, acknowledgment of mistakes will be accompanied by the knowledge of who we can become as our enhanced senses help us to see more clearly the mothers that we may someday be.

Ingredient #3

And now to answer the question of "How can I trust my Heavenly Father more?" The third ingredient for indulging mothers helps with that. We must immerse ourselves in *truth*. We all know and have felt at some point or another what the world thinks about motherhood, but lets make it official. Dr. Shirley Klein, who was introduced in chapter one, asserts that we live in a time where there is a cultural disdain for household work and a social belief that such work limits a woman's full potential. The prevailing attitude is that access to modern conveniences should allow mothers to seek their own fulfillment and that home is a place from which women need to break free. One result of this outlook is that young girls feel it is more appropriate to announce career goals than desires to be wives and mothers.[7]

Elder Bruce Hafen illustrates these feelings in the following story:

> A Latter-day Saint mother who was called to work with young single adults was expecting a new baby. One by one, several of her young women came privately to ask how she really felt about having another child. In a Spirit of deep womanly trust, they asked questions that reflected honest anxiety about being bound to husbands and assuming the burdens of motherhood. She was surprised to hear such concerns from young women who were believing, active Church members. In response, she invited each young woman to do what she had allowed only her husband and children to do. She tenderly placed one of their hands on her abdomen and invited them to feel the baby's movements. Then, with her hand on theirs, she lovingly taught each one that, despite the relentless demands, she had discovered an exquisite happiness through being married and having children. These young women drank with deep reassurance from her well spring of testimony.[8]

Let me add my testimony to that of this Latter-day Saint mother. I not only know of motherhood's importance, but I too know of the exquisite happiness that it brings. For some time, the Spirit directed my path towards specific pursuits. In August 2002, I earned a masters degree from BYU, published a book, and had my sixth baby—all in the same weekend. It was a time when my labors bore all kinds of fruit. I've come to learn that there are many reasons why I needed these experiences in my life, but probably the most important one is so I can testify that the fruits of academic achievement and professional success have all but faded while the fruits of motherhood are sweeter and even more abundant than they have ever been.

Is it any wonder then that prophets and apostles over the years have emphasized the importance of motherhood. President David O. McKay taught that being a mother is a divine calling and is "the greatest trust that has been given to human beings."[9] President Ezra Taft Benson said, "Mothers in Zion, your God given roles are so vital to your own exaltation and to the salvation of your family."[10] From Elder Jeffrey R. Holland we read, "Cherish that role that is so uniquely yours and for which heaven itself sends angels to watch over you and your little ones."[11] And Elder Glen Pace gave strict instructions while speaking at a stake conference I attended to consider "The Family: A Proclamation to the World" as scripture.

All of the above counsel tells us that motherhood is important. Let me use another illustration, also from Elder Hafen, to show you why motherhood is so essential. Elder Hafen writes:

> When first a British colony, Australia was a vast wilderness for exiled convicts. Until 1850, six of every seven Britains who went "down under" were men. And the few women were themselves often convicts or social outcasts. The men ruthlessly exploited them as women without hope, powerless to change their conditions.
>
> In 1840, a reformer named Caroline Chisolm urged that more women would stabilize the culture. She told the British government the best way to establish a "great and good" community in Australia: "for all the clergy you can dispatch, all the schoolmasters you can appoint, all the churches you can build, and all the books you can export, will never do much good without God's police—wives and little children—good and virtuous women."
>
> Chisholm searched for women to raise the moral standard of the people. For twenty years she traveled to England, recruiting young

women and couples who shared the common sense principles of family life. Over time, these women tamed the men who tamed the wild land; and civil society gradually emerged, aided by new state policies that raised women's status and strengthened family life. Eventually, thousands of new immigrants who shared the vision of the good and virtuous women established stable families as the basic unit of Australian society more quickly than had occurred in any other Western country.[12]

The truth of motherhood then is not that the home is a place from which women should escape. The truth is, as Elder Robert D. Hales states, that "the home is the basis of a righteous life, and no other instrumentality can take its place or fulfill its essential functions in carrying forward this God-given responsibility [of motherhood]."[13]

Knowing the truth about motherhood inspires me. It changes my doubt to confidence. It makes me feel less fatigued and more fearless, and I know that my efforts as a mother are far from insignificant—they are heroic. Motherhood becomes a cause that, like the early organizers of Mother's Day activities, I can steadfastly stand behind and promote.

Mixing It All Together

So there are the three ingredients: Unselfishness, Reflection, and Truth. The beauty about this recipe is that they aren't all inclusive. You can take any other gospel truth or principle, add it in, and the result will be the same. But you'll need to make sure that you mix these ingredients together properly. To do this, we'll mix it with *meekness.*

As we do this, it is important to remember that meekness is made up of two important attributes. The first attribute encompasses the way in which most of us look at meekness. Simply said, it means accepting circumstances as they are and patiently enduring the burdens we've been asked to bear. As we look at the second attribute of meekness, however, we see that meekness also means taking righteous action when necessary. The Savior did this when he cleansed the temple or cast out evil spirits. Both attributes of meekness, whether it's enduring patiently or acting courageously, demonstrate a willingness to humbly submit to our Heavenly Father's will. Let's look closer at both attributes of meekness.

The world looks upon meekness as weakness. Elder Maxwell puts forth the following question in his talk "Meekness—a Dimension of True Discipleship." He asks, "Will the world mistake meekness for something else?" He answers his own question by saying, "Yes . . . you live in coarsening times, times in which meekness is both misunderstood and even despised. Yet meekness has been, is, and will remain a nonnegotiable dimension of true discipleship . . . we must not let the world call the cadence for our march through life any more than we would let the world set the direction of that march!"[14] Elder Maxwell continues, "Granted, none of us likes, or should like, to be disregarded, to be silenced, to see a flawed argument prevail, or to endure a gratuitous discourtesy. But such circumstances seldom constitute that field of action from which meekness calls upon us to retire gracefully."[15]

Now think about that. As a mother, have you ever felt disregarded? Have you ever felt silenced? Have you ever watched a flawed argument prevail or experienced a gratuitous discourtesy? I have. But rather than be discouraged by these occurrences, I use them as evidence of my efforts to be meek. As always, we can look to Christ as our example. Was he ever disregarded? Was he silenced? Did He experience gratuitous discourtesy? Yes! More than any other person to sojourn on this earth. But despite the fact that He was mocked and despised, beaten and scourged, and then crucified and encased in a tomb, His power and might could not be repressed. He rose from His tomb on the third day, and paved the way for all mankind to be saved in the mansion of His Father.

The meekness of motherhood is comparable to the meekness of Christ. The work of mothers is mocked. Mothers can feel beaten down by today's trends and attitudes, and the work we do often becomes encased in a tomb of obscurity. But the power of our work cannot be repressed. Joseph F. Smith says this of the power of motherhood:

> Sisters, you do not know how far your influence extends. A mother that is successful in raising a good boy, or girl, to imitate her example and to follow her precepts through life, sows the seeds of virtue, honor and integrity and of righteousness in their hearts that will be felt through all their career in life; and wherever that boy or girl goes, as man or woman, in whatever society they mingle, the good effects

of the example of that mother upon them will be felt; and it will never die, because it well extend from them to their children from generation to generation.[16]

David O. McKay echoes these powerful words:

> Motherhood is the greatest potential influence either for good or ill in human life. The mother's image is the first that stamps itself on the unwritten page of the young child's mind. It is her caress that first awakens a sense of security; her kiss, the first realization of affection; her sympathy and tenderness, the first assurance that there is love in the world . . . that everdirecting and restraining influence implanted during the first years of his childhood linger with him and permeate his thoughts and memory as distinctively as perfume clings to each particular flower.[17]

This brings us to the second attribute of meekness, which is to be meek is also to be mighty. Sometimes that might expresses itself in quiet, almost imperceptible ways as the above quotes illustrate, but meekness can also be exhibited in bold ways. When we consider that many of the mighty acts we read about in the scriptures as well as in Church history come about because an individual selflessly casts aside his or her own personal interests to take up the cause of truth, we must look at these acts of might as being meek as well. Elder Maxwell provides the following examples:

> Moses was once described as being the most meek man on the face of the earth (see Num. 12:3), yet we recall his impressive boldness in the courts of Pharaoh and his scalding indignation following his descent from Sinai.
> President Brigham Young, who was tested in many ways and on many occasions, was once tried in a way that required him to "take it"—even from one he so much adored and admired. Brigham "took it" because he was meek. Yet, surely, none of us sitting here would think of Brigham Young as lacking in boldness or firmness! However, even President Young, in the closing and prestigious days, spent some time in courtrooms being unjustifiably abused. When he might have chosen to assert himself politically, he "took it"—meekly. (See Francis M. Gibbons, Brigham Young: Modern Moses/Prophet of God, [Salt Lake City: Deseret Book Co., 1981], 242-54). . . . A meek, imprisoned Joseph Smith displayed remarkable boldness in rebuking the grossness

of the guards in Richmond jail: "Silence, ye fiends of the infernal pit! In the name of Jesus Christ I rebuke you, and command you to be still; I will not live another minute and hear such language. Cease such talk, or you or I die this instant!" (History of the Church, 3:208).[18]

Of these examples, Elder Maxwell states, "Isn't it interesting that, in a world wrongly impressed with machismo, we see more and more coarseness which is mistaken for manliness, more and more selfishness masquerading as individuality?"[19]

This ability of the world's to masquerade truth is one reason that the meekness of motherhood is not considered mighty. Only recently, I walked into the living room of a dear friend of mine who was pregnant with her fifth child. This friend gets terribly ill when she is pregnant, so she was lying on her couch, in the midst of her four children, doing the best she could to cope with her situation. I looked at her pale face and listened to the concerns she had about being able to endure until she was able to function better. I heard her recount the cruel comments made by those who questioned her choice, and I also listened as she expressed the feelings and impressions that led her to a knowledge of the correctness of her choice, and I thought, "There is courage!"

Another friend, during the 2002 Winter Olympic Games held in Salt Lake City, Utah, was awaiting the arrival of her third child. She recalled that just four years earlier, during the previous winter games, she had just given birth to her first child. Three children in four years! An act of heroism and effort equal to any of the Olympic athletes competing at the time. As we look at these acts of meekness as ones which come about because an individual desires to serve God rather than their own self, these unheralded acts of meekness must also be considered mighty.

One of my favorite books is George Elliott's (pen name for Mary Ann Evans) *Middlemarch*. In it, Dorothea Brooke is a young, serious minded woman who has great plans for changing and improving the world. As she seeks to accomplish her grand ambitions, she is met with emptiness and discouragement. As she searches for fulfillment, she ultimately finds it building a life with a man based on genuine love. George Elliott describes Dorothea's initial ambitions as "the mixed result of young and noble impulse struggling amidst the conditions of an imperfect social state, in which great feelings will often take the aspect of error, and great faith the aspect of illusion."[20] As Dorothea gives up her ambitions of error and illusion and meekly falls into the role of wife and mother, she is described in this oft quoted statement: "Her finely-touched spirit had still its fine issues, though they were not widely visible. Her full nature, like the river of which Cyrus broke the strength, spent itself in channels which had no great name on the earth. But the effect of her being on those around her was incalculably diffusive: for the growing good of the world is partly dependent on unhistoric acts; and that things are not so ill with you and me as they might have been is half owing to the number who lived faithfully a hidden life, and rest in unvisited tombs."[21]

With these compelling beliefs driving the theme and plot of *Middlemarch,* it is not surprising that Mary Ann Evans had this to say about motherhood. Consider her words in the context of our discussion about meekness and might: "Mighty is the force of motherhood! It transforms all things by its vital heat; it turns timidity into fierce courage, and dreadless defiance into tremulous submission; it turns thoughtlessness into foresight, and yet stills all anxiety into calm content; it makes selfishness become self-denial, and gives even to hard vanity the glance of admiring love."[22]

You can see, then, that as we turn our backs on the world's perception that meekness is a form a weakness, and as we embrace the truth that to be meek is ultimately to be mighty, meekness becomes an essential element for turning our recipe of denial into one of indulgence.

A Mother Heart

The result of our recipe is taking shape. We've added our ingredients: unselfishness, reflection, and truth. We've mixed those ingredients with meekness, and as you can see, what we have ultimately created is a *mother heart*!

Julie Beck, General Relief Society President, defines a "mother heart" beautifully in a talk given to the Young Women of the Church. She first asks, "What is a mother heart and how is one acquired?" She then responds by saying:

> We learn about some of those qualities in the scriptures. To

paraphrase Proverbs: "Who can find a . . . woman [with a mother heart]? for her price is far above rubies . . . She . . . worketh willingly with her hands. . . . With the fruit of her hands she planteth a vineyard . . . she stretcheth out her hand to the poor . . . Strength and honour are her clothing . . . She openeth her mouth with wisdom; and in her tongue is the law of kindness. She looketh well to the ways of her household, and eateth not the bread of idleness" (Proverbs 31:10, 13, 16, 20, 25–27). A woman with a mother heart has a testimony of the restored gospel, and she teaches the principles of the gospel without equivocation. She is keeping sacred covenants made in holy temples. Her talents and skills are shared unselfishly. She gains as much education as her circumstances will allow, improving her mind and spirit with the desire to teach what she learns to the generations who follow her.

. . . She is a "goodly parent" (1 Nephi 1:1) who lives and teaches standards of behavior exactly in line with the teachings of living prophets. She teaches her "children to pray and to walk uprightly before the Lord" (D&C 68:28). Rather than listening to the voices and partial truths of the world, she knows that gospel standards are based on eternal, unchangeable truths. She believes that to be "primarily responsible for the nurture of [her] children" is a vital, dignified, and "sacred responsibilit[y]" ("The Family: A Proclamation to the World," Ensign, Nov. 1995, p. 102). To nurture and feed them physically is as much an honor as to nurture and feed them spiritually. She is "not weary of well doing" and delights to serve her family, because she knows that "out of small things proceedeth that which is great" (D&C 64:33).[23]

We hear praise for those around us who have a "surgeon's hands," an "artist's eye," a "head for figures," or the "touch of a musician." All of these compliments seem to pale somewhat in comparison to Sister Beck's description of a "mother heart."

In her talk, Sister Beck gives examples of women with "mother hearts." One of these examples is Sister Beck's own mother. She explains:

> I have often heard my father describe my mother as a woman with a "mother heart," and that is true. Her mothering influence has been felt by many hundreds, perhaps thousands of people, and she has refined the role of nurturer to an art form. Her testimony of the restored gospel of Jesus Christ and strong sense of identity and purpose have guided her life.
>
> She took longer than most women to find her husband, but during

her single years she devoted her life to progress. Though it was uncommon at the time, she was university educated and advancing in a career. Following her marriage, children arrived in quick succession; and in a short span of years, she was the mother of a large family. All the knowledge she had acquired, all her natural abilities and gifts, all her skills were channeled into an organization that had no earthly bounds. As a covenant-keeping daughter of God, she had prepared all her life for motherhood.[24]

Sister Beck also describes a group of women she met at a park as having "mother hearts." Of these women, she says,

> They were young, covenant-keeping women. They were bright and had obtained advanced degrees from respected universities. Now they were devoting their considerable gifts to planning dinner that evening and sharing housekeeping ideas. They were teaching two-year-olds to be kind to one another. They were soothing babies, kissing bruised knees, and wiping tears. I asked one of those mothers how it came about that she could transfer her talents so cheerfully into the role of motherhood. She replied, "I know who I am, and I know what I am supposed to do. The rest just follows." That young mother will build faith and character in the next generation one family prayer at a time, one scripture study session, one book read aloud, one song, one family meal after another. She is involved in a great work. She knows that "children are an heritage of the Lord" and "happy is the [woman] that hath [a] quiver full of them" (Psalm 127:3, 5). She knows that the influence of righteous, conscientious, persistent, daily mothering is far more lasting, far more powerful, far more influential than any earthly position or institution invented by man. She has the vision that, if worthy, she has the potential to be blessed as Rebekah of old to be "the mother of thousands of millions" (Genesis 24:60).[25]

In Sister Beck's definition and examples of women with "mother hearts," I can see the result of our recipe. I can sense the blessings of unselfishness that come into the lives of mothers. I can feel the spirit directing mother's paths. And I can see the truth lifting mothers above the fleeting and ever changing attitudes of the world. As the young mother in the park said, a mother heart helps us to know who we are and to know what we are supposed to do. Certainty and faith in a world full of doubt and fear is indeed an indulgence.

But with this "mother heart" comes two other amazing indulgences.

Just as this recipe helps us as mothers see who we really are, it also helps us to see who our children really are. And as we come to see ourselves and our children more clearly, we also come to know Christ better. So let's look at the deeper knowledge of our children and a clearer knowledge of Christ as part of the sweet smells and tastes of this recipe.

Knowledge of Children

C. S. Lewis' books *The Chronicles of Narnia* can be considered the most celebrated children's literature of all time. The first book that C. S. Lewis wrote for the series, *The Lion, the Witch, and the Wardrobe*, is perhaps the most well known and oft-read of the series. Multiple screen and stage adaptations have been made of this story where four children, Peter, Susan, Edmund, and Lucy Pevensie, find their way into a magical land called Narnia. Once there, they join Aslan, a magnificent and wise lion, in an attempt to free Narnia from the grasps of the tyrannical White Witch.

In 2006 Walden Media produced a film adaptation of this story titled *The Chronicles of Narnia*. This film begins by depicting the terrifying bombings of London in World War II. Because of these bombings, thousands of children were sent to live with sponsors in the country in order to preserve their lives from the destruction. Following an intense bombing scene, the film portrays an overcrowded railway station where hundreds of children, including the Pevensies, have labels pinned onto their clothing. These labels are meant to assist the children in getting to their proper destinations in the country.

When Peter, Susan, Edmund, and Lucy are dropped off at the railway station designated by their labels, they find it deserted. Nervous and unsure as to what to do, Edmund looks at his tag and says, "Perhaps we've been incorrectly labeled." What ensues from this point, is a journey where the children will discover that they have indeed been mislabeled—not physically mislabeled, for they are at the correct railway station. But they have been mislabeled in the sense that neither they nor many of the people they meet see or understand who they really are.

For example, after a short wait at the deserted railway station, Mrs.

Macready, the housekeeper of the country estate where the children will be staying, arrives to pick them up. She is a severe looking woman, and she asks them curtly, "Is this it then? Haven't you brought anything else?" Peter then replies, "No mum. It's just us." Mrs. Macready then scrutinizes the children before saying sardonically, "Small favors."

"Small favors." A label hardly worthy of the children who will be known in the land of Narnia as the "Sons of Adam" and the "Daughters of Eve"—the two human boys and the two human girls who will become the future kings and queens of Narnia. The children, themselves, accept the label of "small favors" more readily than they accept the label of "kings and queens." But through their incredible journey through Narnia, they discover the "kings and queens" inside themselves. Aslan, the majestic lion who is seen by many as a type and shadow of Christ in the story, ultimately gives the children their final labels. Once the battle with the White Witch has been won, a glorious coronation ceremony is held where Lucy, Edmund, Susan, and Peter take their rightful places as kings and queens of Narnia. Aslan presents the children to the cheering crowd and proclaims, "I give you Queen Lucy the Valiant. I give you King Edmund the Just. I give you Queen Susan the Gentle. And I give you King Peter the Magnificent." As the subjects of Narnia continue to cheer, Aslan decrees, "Once a king or queen of Narnia, always a king or queen of Narnia!"

Our own children live in a world where they are frequently labeled improperly by both those around them as well as by themselves. It is our privilege as mothers to recognize and give our children their proper labels—to stand in the place of Christ and help them understand that they have the potential to become future kings and queens throughout all eternity. As mothers, as we come to see the power and worth and majesty of motherhood, the power, worth, and majesty of our children becomes infinitely more clear.

If you'll indulge me, I'd like to introduce you to my own children and share with you the labels my husband and I, with the help of the Spirit, have given them so far:

First, I give you my oldest son, "Christian the Clever and Charismatic!" Few people I know have a memory like Christian's. He remembers everything, especially where the gospel is concerned. He can answer scripture questions as though he's been a scripture scholar for years. I'd like to take some credit for this, but I can't. We are just like any other family as far as scripture study is concerned. We go in spurts, but it is enough for Christian to wow seminary teachers and Church leaders alike with his knowledge of the gospel. He is also a great thinker and communicator, and he has that natural quality of leadership that draws people to him. He has always been social and accepting of others. When he was a small baby, just barely talking yet old enough to sit in a shopping cart, we would walk up and down the aisles of the grocery store and he would say, "Hi guys! Doing?" to anyone who passed. Of course, everyone responded favorably to this cute little friendly baby, and people continue to respond favorably to him today. Like any teenager, he has his struggles. But when he is at home, I am able to remind him of his talents and strengths and instill within him the courage he'll need to successfully navigate in the world.

We call our second son, Caleb, "Sparkle Boy!" This is because everything about him sparkles. His eyes and his countenance sparkle with his genuinely happy and easygoing personality. His mind sparkles with intelligence. His body sparkles with athleticism. His efforts sparkle with determination and endurance. His spirit sparkles with insight and understanding. And whenever he is at home, we all sparkle with laughter because of his sense of humor. Caleb's quick wit has amused us since he was very young. When he was a toddler, we laughed with him at the dinner table where he would pull faces at himself in the reflection of the microwave door. When he was a preschooler, we laughed with him when he played good natured tricks on his preschool friends. As he got older, we always counted on his clever comebacks in otherwise ordinary situations to keep us on our toes. Of course, as a teenage boy, with several younger siblings, he often uses this talent for humor to tease and torment, so I have to remind him to use his powers for good and not for evil! Ultimately, I know he will as I see him "sparkling" not only in our home but in school, in Scouts, in sports, and in Church as well.

Next, I give you "Jeremiah the Steady, Stalwart, and Stellar!" As a sixth grader, Jeremy won the Hope of America award. I was privileged to introduce him at the awards ceremony where I used these three words to describe him. He is steady because he does all the things he has been asked to do and all the things he has chosen to do with willing hands and a happy heart. He is stalwart because even when his undertakings become difficult or challenging, he works hard to overcome the challenges and accomplish the tasks before him. And he is stellar because that is the natural result of working with happy hands and a willing heart and seeing things through to the end. And the result of Jeremy's work is just that. He is a stellar student. He is a stellar athlete. He is a stellar musician. He is a stellar Scout. And most importantly, he is a stellar son. If I ever say, "Will someone go get me this particular item?" or "Can somebody do that particular task for me?" Jeremy is the one who always does it. As he gets older, he is beginning to show insight, thoughtfulness, and independence in accomplishing both what is asked of him as well as what isn't, and this independence of thinking will continue to propel him towards stellar results.

After three sons, our family was blessed with a daughter. My husband and I named her Ariel for the city of Jerusalem (see Isaiah 29:1) where he and I met as students. So I give you "Ariel the Spontaneous and Creative." Ariel has such a bright mind and is keenly intelligent. She generates ideas and makes connections at an alarmingly rapid pace. I look on in awe as she moves from one creative act to another, working in all sorts of different mediums: she writes, she reads, she sings, she sketches, she dabbles in architecture, design, and fashion, and she is also a fine actress. The result of all this energy and ambition is a highly focused and clear thinking mind. In family council, we never need to fear being short on input from our children because Ariel's creative solutions to problems keep everyone alert and attentive. Ariel is a solid and levelheaded young lady, who makes the right decisions for the right reasons because her ability to think things through always brings her to the truth, which is what the gospel is firmly rooted in. She is a fine example of a daughter of God, and we are blessed to have that example in our home.

Only one word is needed to describe our fourth son and fifth child, so with that said, I give you "Seth the Exuberant!" The word exuberant describes Seth in every way. It describes his spirit, which is infused with energy and enthusiasm. It describes his countenance, which is clean, pure, bright, and highlighted with just a splash a freckles across his nose. It describes his personality, which bursts with cheer and excitement. It describes his level of energy, which is lively and high-spirited. It describes how he communicates, which resounds with eagerness and zeal. And it describes how affectionate he is. When Seth smiles at me with his shining eyes and that splash of freckles, there is just something magnetic about him, and we usually end up in a big bear hug. As I squeeze Seth tightly, I am able to remind him that Heavenly Father loves him more than I do, and that He is just as eager to embrace Seth in this same way one day.

After having five children in seven years, I needed a little breather, so we took a four year break from babies. But once that break was over, we welcomed into our home our sixth child and fifth son, Micah. From very early on, Micah was highly communicative. He spoke early, as many children do, but Micah began speaking with an awareness of language and its workings that was remarkable for one so young. When he was only two years old, he described his bath not just as hot but as spicy hot. Anything soft was as soft as a cloud, and he didn't just become dizzy, he became dizzy as a merry-go-round. I was amazed at Micah's ability to be speaking in similes so early. With that said, I give you "Micah the Articulate and Industrious." As Micah grows older, his awareness of language increases, and he becomes more verbal and more articulate. This awareness for the details that make up language and communication serves as a catalyst for his industriousness. Micah is simply a very hard worker. He understands tasks, and he also has the ability to determine what must be done to accomplish that task. Then he does what it takes to complete that task. He proceeds in his work with a quiet determination that would be impressive in one much older than he. As it presents itself in one so young, I can't help but see a powerful and indomitable leader emerging to serve in our Heavenly Father's kingdom.

Bethany is our seventh child and second daughter. We call her our "Effervescent Sprite!" Her personality bubbles with vivacity and energy. She loves life and approaches situations with excitement and animation. She has long blonde flowing hair that is a touch on the unruly side, but when she runs through the yard with the sun shining on her face and the wind blowing through her hair, she epitomizes joy and she reminds me what it truly means to enjoy the journey. A sprite is a diminutive, supernatural being who has the power to intervene in the lives of others. Bethany has definitely come into our home and given us a greater power to obtain happiness. She is a small child and has the faith of a small child, which shines through in her vibrancy. In this, I see clearly that when we are full of faith we cannot help but to approach life with eagerness and hope, and Bethany's spirit spills over with hope. Her natural ability to be faithful and hopeful helps her to be purely happy. Being around that kind of happiness helps me to wash all my worries away. In fact, one of my goals each day is to laugh with Bethany, because when I do that, I become more connected to the happiness I know Heavenly Father wants for me.

Presenting my children to you makes me want to shout from the rooftops, "I am the mother of these amazing kids! They are future kings and queens, gods and goddesses! I know this to be true, because I know each one of them so intimately. I am their mother and know and believe in their nobility. This gives me a surer knowledge of the nobility of my work as a mother."

I understand why Christ would give so much, even His very life, for my children. I know why He shows so much love for them, because I get to feel that Christlike love for them daily. I understand why Christ believes in my children, because I get to watch firsthand their miraculous progression and growth. And I know that this belief in and love for my children is why Christ sacrificed so much in order to lead the way for us to follow Him back to our Heavenly Father. And so it is that coming to understand the importance and power of motherhood, helps me to come to a greater understanding of Christ.

Knowledge of Christ

Elder James E. Talmage taught, "the world's greatest champion of woman and womanhood is Jesus the Christ."[26] During the time of Christ's life, a woman's status in society was considered barely above that of a slave. Women were rarely educated and interaction with men (other than her husband) of any kind was forbidden. But even if it meant challenging the current social practices of the day, Christ desired to raise the status of women. Thus, at a public well, he taught a woman about living water. And he invited not only Mary, but Martha, to put aside domestic duties and learn at his feet.[27] Today we live in a world where women are much freer to pursue paths to help us reach our full potential. But that same world misleads us about what that potential should be. Again, Christ is willing to challenge the current social practices of the day to show us our true potential and raise us to it.

Listen to how Jack Christiansen in his landmark talk, "Women of Light" testifies of the true potential of women:

> If all things bear record of Christ, then women bear record of Christ. Sisters, you are perhaps the ultimate symbol of the Son of God . . .
>
> As God teaches us, "That by reason of transgression cometh the fall, which fall bringeth death, and inasmuch as ye were born into the world by water, and blood, and the spirit, which I have made, and so became of dust a living soul, even so ye must be born again into the kingdom of heaven, of water, and of the Spirit, and be cleansed by blood, even the blood of mine Only Begotten; that ye might be sanctified from all sin, and enjoy the words of eternal life in this world, and eternal life in the world to come, even immortal glory; For by the water ye keep the commandment; by the spirit ye are justified, and by the blood ye are sanctified" (Moses 6: 59-60).
>
> Now sisters, why are you a symbol of Christ? As we've learned from this scripture, the dust of the earth is water, blood, and spirit. What three elements are present when a child is born? They are water, blood, and spirit. As Jesus shed His blood to give spiritual life and eternal life, what then is the role of those who have the opportunity to be mothers? They shed their very life's blood to give physical, mortal life. And so the birth process—how we all enter this world—is literally a symbol of being born again, a symbol of the Son of God shedding His blood. In fact, Elder Matthew Cowley, a former member of the Quorum of the Twelve apostles, said this: "You sisters belong to the great sorority of Saviorhood. You may not hold the priesthood. Men are different, men have to have something given to them to make them saviors of men, but not mothers, not women. You are born with an inherent right, an inherent ability, to be the saviors of human souls. You are the co-creators with God of His children. Therefore, it is expected of you by a right divine that you be the saviors and the regenerating force

in the lives of God's children here upon the earth" (*Matthew Cowley Speaks,* 1976, 109).[28]

Brother Christiansen concludes by saying, "You, as women... belong to the sorority of Saviorhood. I don't know if I have heard anything more beautiful than that."[29] And I say, what could be more decadent and indulgent than the truth found in that quote? Cook or no cook, I know a good recipe when I taste one!

Recipes for delicious food are passed around and shared because they not only nourish our bodies, they make us feel something. I've observed people eagerly asking for and writing down a recipe in hopes of not only duplicating the taste of the dish, but the feelings it generated as well. It is not only our duty but our privilege to share this recipe with others, and most important, to our daughters.

Consider the experience former General Young Women's President, Susan W. Tanner, had with her daughter:

> Several years ago my husband and I asked our children what they liked about the recent general conference. Our then 16-year-old daughter was elated. She said, "I loved it! I loved hearing inspired, intelligent prophets and leaders affirm motherhood." Then she told us that this was one of the disturbing anxieties in her life: "I just don't hear it from anyone — not at seminary, not in Young Women, and definitely not at school; nowhere except at home."[30]

Sister Tanner then observed similar feelings from a large group of Laurels when discussing their goals with them. She recalls,

> The first few mentioned educational goals such as getting a PhD; some said they would like to go on a mission—all worthy goals. Finally one girl timidly expressed the desire to be a mother. Then a few more girls talked about other goals. After one more girl mentioned motherhood, the rest of them joined in. But is was quite courageous for those first two girls to admit they wanted to be mothers. And this was in a very safe setting.[31]

If in very safe environments, like Young Women and seminary, and even church classrooms, our daughters are not being nourished and nurtured regarding the truth of motherhood. We as mothers need to be sure they are getting double helpings of it at home. And if we are leaders and teachers of young women of all ages, we need to share this recipe with them in abundance. After all, this recipe is not fattening, it won't clog any arteries, or make cholesterol climb. Instead, it will touch hearts, strengthen resolve and expand spirits. Best of all, it will open lines of communication, because good recipes, like this one, hold within them the power to unify.

One young mother experienced the unifying power of truth when her small daughter eagerly asked to be taught. She recalls:

> One afternoon Katelyn announced it was time to go to church, and her two favorite dolls were ready to put on their pretty dresses . . . Katelyn informed me that "church" was inside our large plastic playhouse and suggested we go inside.
>
> After nestling her dolls in a corner, Katelyn settled herself and then looked up at me with large, eager eyes. "Teach me, Mommy," she said. Delighted at the opportunity to capitalize on this moment, I jumped right into my role as "teacher." I told some stories about Jesus and then sang a few familiar Primary songs. Leery of overextending my daughter's invitation to be taught and driven by an assumption that she would quickly tire of my instruction, I soon ended our discussion.
>
> But once again those bright eyes turned up to me as she implored, "Teach me, Mommy." Surprised by her attention span, I stepped it up a notch. . . She listened attentively and at each pause, she would once again request, "Teach me, Mommy."
>
> There we sat, my toddler, her dolls, and me, inside our playhouse, talking about the truths of eternity. Although she was the one who requested to be taught, I am certain that I learned a lesson, too.[32]

Like this mother, I have learned so many "truths of eternity" as I focused on my children, and one of these truths has been that the seeming denials of motherhood are ultimately indulgences. The experiences that have led me to this truth have come about because I was willing to look at motherhood not as confining but as freeing. I was able to trust in Heavenly Father' plan for me and find myself in the world of my children. I have come to embrace the well-known scripture, "He that loseth his life for my sake shall find it" (Matthew 10:39).

So use this recipe of the "Indulgent Denial of Motherhood" often and regularly. As you use generous portions of unselfishness, reflection, and truth, and as you mix these ingredients with meekness, you will develop more and more the "mother heart" spoken of by Sister Beck. You will also come to know your children as Christ knows them. You will draw closer to Christ, and you will also draw closer to the woman Heavenly Father knows you can be.

Notes

1. Neal A. Maxwell, "Becoming a Disciple," *Ensign,* June 1996, 16.
2. "Mother's Day," 123Holiday, http://mothers-day.123holiday.net/index/html.
3. Neal A. Maxwell, "The Precious Promise," *The Rock of Our Redeemer: Talks from the 2002 BYU Women's Conference* (Salt Lake City: Deseret Book, 2003), 5.
4. Ibid.
5. "Mother's Day," 123Holiday, http://mothers-day.123holiday.net/index/html.
6. James E. Faust, "The Gift of the Holy Ghost—A Sure Compass," *Ensign,* May 1989, 31.
7. Klein, "Preserving the Sacred Home," 56–57.
8. Bruce Hafen, *The Touch of Human Kindness* (Salt Lake City: Eagle Gate, 2000), 1.
9. David O. McKay, *The Responsibility of Parents to Their Children* (pamphlet, n.d.), 1.
10. Ezra Taft Benson, from an address at a fireside for parents on 22 February 1987).
11. Jeffrey R. Holland, "Because She Is a Mother," *Ensign*, May 1997, 35–37.
12. Hafen, *The Touch of Human Kindness*, 12–13.
13. Robert D. Hales, "Strengthening Families: Our Sacred Duty," *Ensign*, May 1999, 32–34.
14. Neal A. Maxwell, "Meekness—a Dimension of True Discipleship," *Ensign*, Mar. 1983, 70.
15. Ibid.
16. *Teachings of Presidents of the Church: Joseph F. Smith,* (Salt Lake City: The Church of Jesus Christ of Latter-day Saints, 1998), 32.
17. *Teachings of Presidents of the Church: David O. McKay* (Salt Lake City: The Church of Jesus Christ of Latter-day Saints, 2003), 156.
18. Neal A. Maxwell, "Meekness—a Dimension of True Discipleship," *Ensign*, Mar. 1983, 70.
19. Ibid.

20. George Elliot, *Middlemarch,* (New York: Modern Library Edition, 1994), 798–99.
21. Ibid.
22. Mary Ann Evans, *Thoughts on Being a Mother* (New York: Exley, 1998), npn.
23. Julie B. Beck, "A Mother Heart," *Ensign,* May 2004, 75–77.
24. Ibid.
25. Ibid.
26. James E. Talmage, *Jesus the Christ* (Salt Lake City: Deseret Book, 1997), 475.
27. Blair G. Van Dyke "Sorting Out the Seven Women Named Mary in the New Testament," *The Religious Educator,* v. 5 n. 3, 2004, 57.
28. *To Mother, With Love,* 10–11.
29. Ibid.
30. Susan W. Tanner, "Strengthening Future Mothers," *Ensign,* June 2005, 20.
31. Ibid.
32. Karsen Cranney, "Teach Me, Mommy," *Ensign,* June 2005, 25.

3
The Exhilarating Exhaustion of Motherhood

Journal Entry: August 4, 1997

Wow! There's a lot to report about the happenings of the last two months. The first and most important is that it's time for us to welcome another baby into our home. I really couldn't believe it when I first felt the Spirit's promptings. I'm pretty sure I said out loud to anyone who might be listening, "What? Are you crazy?!" It's not surprising then that I pushed the prompting aside and completely ignored it. But it wasn't long before the Spirit whispered again—this time as I listened to the messages of Sister Workman, (the Mount Timpanogos temple matron), Janet Lee (wife of late BYU president Rex Lee), and singer/songwriter Deanna Edwards—they were speaking at "wives day" for seminary teachers.

Each of their messages held one common thread for me, which can be summed up in one word: bargain. All three spoke of petitioning the Lord in prayer and then realizing that they had a part to play in receiving an answer. All of the prayers spoken of were answered in ways that filled each woman's heart with great joy and peace. That is the Lord's way. He always lives up to his end of the bargain, and each of these women truly went the extra mile to do her part—to live up to her end of the bargain. As I sat and listened and felt the spirit and cried tears of joy right along with the speakers, the whispering to welcome another baby into our home came again. This time I embraced the idea realizing that it is how I can do my part, and I left the meeting feeling inspired and energized.

Each husband had written his wife a letter, so I took mine and drove to the grounds of the Mount Timpanogos temple to read it. Blair is always so kind and eloquent and loving in his notes and cards, and this letter was no different. Reading it helped to reaffirm all the feelings I'd had at the meeting and made me feel even more at peace. I couldn't wait to tell Blair the news, but he was in Alaska so it would have to wait.

The wind was blowing very hard that reminded me of home and Mom—an appropriate connection to feel at the time. I watched the wind blow the flowers planted so beautifully in the temple gardens. There are so many different varieties, and all the different flowers made me think of children—all different but beautiful in their own way. Just as I got up to leave, the sprinklers came on and sprayed me before I could move. But the wind and the water gave me such a refreshing burst that I felt connected to everything around me: the earth, the temple, home, and Heavenly Father. It's been a long time since I've felt that much joy and peace!

But an interesting thing happened once I got back home to sleepless nights and noisy kids. I started rationalizing that the Lord couldn't possibly mean now. Perhaps a few months from now. Surely not right this very minute now. And when Blair got home I was really mad at him for really no reason at all. But the longer he was home the madder I became, and I thought, "I can't have another baby. I don't even like my husband." But then Blair shared with me an experience he had in Alaska, which taught the principle that after a spiritual experience comes temptation, and I immediately knew why I hated my husband for no reason—I was being tempted. And with this realization came reconciliation, but I still thought that the spirit couldn't possibly mean I should have a baby right this minute, and so the story continues . . .

Very shortly after this, Blair and I went to another meeting for seminary teachers and their wives. At the meeting, the speaker related the story of how he dreamed of two little girls, both tall like their mother. One had black hair while the other had blonde hair. He'd had this dream when they were expecting their fifth child. He and his wife had previously decided that they would have six children, so after the dream, they both anticipated a dark haired girl. Well, the baby came and it was a boy, and baby #6 came, and it was a boy. And the husband told this wife that he couldn't even say the word seven without gagging, but his dream of the two beautiful girls was still very poignant to him. So baby #7 came along and it was a girl with a

Unlikely Truths of Motherhood

full head of black hair. And baby #8 came along and it was a bald headed baby girl with just a bit of blonde fuzz.

It was during the relating of this story that the Spirit assured me that all would be well if I would just have faith in the Lord's timetable . . . so I decided I would! What a patient loving Heavenly Father! I feel so grateful and blessed to have been led down such a path of understanding and inspiration, but that's not the end of the story.

I am so tired! But what's new about that? And after a trip to Idaho with just me and the kids for a week while Blair remodeled, and after an extended visit in Ogden for two days while Blair continued to remodel, and after walking into a remodeling disaster area when we finally did get home, and after Blair's three-day trip to Texas that left me and the kids living in the remodeling disaster, and after the TV broke down that left me feeling just a little ashamed to find out how much I depend on the stupid thing, and after a day of church, which is always a struggle to get through with four small children while your husband is at meetings all day . . . well, after all this, I sat down after church to get my bearings when the fast offering collectors came. And while I was writing out the check, something inside of me said, "Why are you doing this?" Not referring to the check, but to all of it, including the check. The words loyalty, habit, and tradition came to mind but none of these words satisfied me. So when the fast offering collectors went away, I sat down even more frustrated than before. But later, as I watched a program about the Church members who reenacted the pioneers trek west, the right word came to me: faith! I realized just what "faith in every footstep" means. Not just faith in the big footsteps like those that carry you through a riverbed or help you decide to have another baby. But faith in every footstep including the ones on flat level ground and the ones that find you paying fast offerings and sending your husband off to meetings. It's faith in the bigger, broader vision—the vision that tells the pioneers as they enter a dry desolate land that "the desert shall blossom like a rose." So I will work on my faith although I am still tired, but like I said before, "What's new about that?" And that is the end of the story.

The title of this chapter is "Exhilarating Exhaustion." And like the above journal entry where a series of exhausting experiences brought me to an exhilarating end, I'm expecting that this chapter's sequences will do the same for us. One of my favorite hymns is "Be Still, My Soul" and one of my favorite lines in that hymn is "Be still my soul, thy best, thy heavenly friend, through thorny paths leads to a joyful end." Exhilarating exhaustion is just that—the work and toil you go through in order to achieve a "joyful end." It's no surprise then that motherhood, with its endless service and sacrifice, brings into women's lives more joyful ends than anything else that can be undertaken.

In this chapter, we'll talk about six Christlike characteristics that mothers develop as we serve and sacrifice for our children. They are: faith, strength, submission, hope, charity, and discernment. While each of these characteristics are joyful ends in and of themselves, taken together, they lead us on a progressive journey that helps us to understand more fully the power inherent in motherhood. These six Christlike characteristics, in fact, enable us to take our initial steps into motherhood with faith, perhaps not even understanding why we are doing the things we've been asked to do, but they enable us to end our journey with discernment, which is the ability to see with spiritual eyes the exhilaration that comes not only into our children's lives but into our lives as well as we focus on motherhood.

Faith

In my journal entry, when I finally realized that faith was the force that was keeping me moving, I declared, "and that is the end of the story." But in actuality, faith was just the beginning. It was the impetus I needed to enter into yet another stage of motherhood. And in most of our lives, as we strive to do the right thing, faith is the beginning. It is that first step into what is often an unknown. Elder Boyd K. Packer learned this principle regarding faith from President Harold B. Lee. Elder Packer had been counseled by President David O. McKay regarding a problem he was having. Elder Packer confided in President Lee that he saw no way he could move in the direction President McKay had counseled him to go. President Lee then said the following to Elder Packer: "The trouble with you is you want to see the end from the beginning . . . you must learn to walk to the edge of the light, and then a few steps into the darkness, then the light will appear and show the way before you." Elder Packer called this counsel from President Lee a "lesson of a lifetime."[1]

Once the light has appeared to show us the way, it will not light our entire course. It will only light the portion of it that Heavenly Father wants us to see. It still requires faith to continue on our path trusting in Heavenly Father's vision and perspective. Elder James E. Talmage illustrates this point with an experience he calls, "The Parable of the Owl Express." Elder Talmage was a young college student who had been out in the field doing some work with a geology class. A sudden and fierce snow storm caused them to halt their work early, and they made their way to a little train station hoping to find a ride home. They learned the train that was stopping that night had been held up by the storm and would get to the station late. Long after midnight, the train finally arrived, but while his companions boarded the train immediately, Elder Talmage was drawn to the engineer who was busily inspecting and making adjustments to the train. He approached him and asked him how he felt on such a night, "wild, weird, and furious, when the powers of destruction seemed to be let loose, abroad and uncontrolled, when the storm was howling and when danger threatened from every side."

Elder Talmage recalls that the answer was a lesson not to be forgotten. In effect, the engineer said, "Look at the engine headlight. Doesn't that light up the track for a hundred yards or more? Well, all I try to do is to cover that hundred yards of lighted track. That I can see, and for that distance I know the roadbed is open and safe . . . Believe me, I have never been able to drive this old engine of mine so fast as to outstrip that hundred yards of lighted track. The light is always ahead of me."[2]

From this experience, Elder Talmage learned, "We may not know what lies ahead of us in the future years, nor even in the days or hours immediately beyond. But for a few yards, or possibly only a few feet, the track is clear, our duty is plain, our course is illumined. For that short distance, for the next step, lighted by the inspiration of God, go on!"[3]

So with regards to motherhood, what are those first steps we are required to take in faith? President Hinckley illumined them beautifully when he said,

Some years ago President Benson delivered a message to the women of the Church. He encouraged them to leave their employment and give their individual time to their children. I sustain the position he took. Nevertheless, I recognize as he recognized, that there are some women who have to work to provide for the needs of their families. To you I say, do the very best you can. I hope that if you are employed full-time you are doing it to ensure that basic needs are met and not simply to indulge a taste for an elaborate home, fancy cars, and other luxuries. The greatest job that any mother will ever do will be in nurturing, teaching, lifting, encouraging, and rearing her children in righteousness and truth. None other can adequately take her place. It is well nigh impossible to be full-time homemaker and full-time employee. . . to the mothers of the Church, every mother who is here today, I want to say that as the years pass, you will become increasingly grateful for that which you did in molding the lives of your children in the direction of righteousness and goodness, integrity, and faith. That is most likely to happen if you can spend adequate time with them.[4]

. . . And so I plead with you tonight, my dear sisters. Sit down and quietly count the debits and the credits in your role as a mother. It is not too late. When all else fails, there is prayer and the promised help of the Lord to assist you in your trials. But do not delay. Start now, whether your child is 6 or 16.[5]

I am so grateful for President Hinckley's testimony of the importance of motherhood. I am grateful for the challenge he gave us as mothers to put our children first. In a darkened world where messages of self saturate the prevailing attitudes towards motherhood, I am grateful for the light shone by President Hinckley in his lifetime.

I am also grateful for the powerful testimony our current prophet, President Thomas S. Monson, bears of motherhood. He testifies, "May each of us treasure this truth: One cannot forget mother and remember God. One cannot remember mother and forget God. Why? Because these two sacred persons, God and mother, partners in creation, in love, in sacrifice, in service, are as one."[6]

This powerful light of testimony is important to me because I sometimes succumb to the darkened and distorted messages of the world. I sometimes feel sorry for myself that I lack prestige and position that a woman with my education and experience could have in the working world. I sometimes resent the budget restraints that I have to adhere to because I have no occupation to bring in extra money. I sometimes pity myself and wonder if the sacrifices I make as a mother are of worth. But when I read about the importance of motherhood, when I listen to talks regarding the eternal rewards of motherhood, when I hear the testimonies of prophets both past and present, the light of truth illumines my path, and I am able to press forward with faith once more.

As mothers, we are blessed to have scriptural accounts of two faithful women who pressed forward with faith even when their paths were illumined only a little at the onset of their journeys into motherhood. Those women are Mary, the mother of Jesus, and Elisabeth, the mother of John.

S. Kent Brown, a professor of Ancient Scripture at BYU, wrote a beautiful book entitled *Mary and Elisabeth: Noble Daughter's of God*. In it, we learn that Mary's first reaction to the news that she would soon be the mother of the Son of God was fear. We know this because in the angel Gabriel's initial greeting he pleads, "Fear not, Mary" (Luke 1:30). He must have sensed her fear and knew that she was "troubled" (Luke 1:29). In Greek, "troubled" means "thoroughly frightened" or "thoroughly upset."[7] But Gabriel calmed Mary's heart and prepared her to receive his astonishing message about her coming motherhood. He declared, "Behold, thou shalt conceive in thy womb, and bring forth a son, and shalt call his name Jesus. He shall be great, and shall be called the Son of the Highest" (Luke 1:31–32).

Regarding this announcement, Brother Brown writes of Mary:

> At this moment of moments, when heaven was announcing the long-awaited arrival of Christ, one emotion did not overpower Mary's heart: self-doubt. It is a measure of both her righteousness and resilience that she did not let her fears or doubts overcome her. Instead, . . . she had the presence of mind to ask a penetrating question: "How shall this be, seeing I know not a man?" (Luke 1:34). She did not disbelieve Gabriel's promise of a child. . . . Rather, she was trying hard to grasp the meaning of his message. Mary's question focused on the "how" of the promised child's coming, not "if" he would be born.[8]

To Mary's question, Gabriel answered, "The Holy Ghost shall come upon thee, and the power of the Highest shall overshadow thee . . . that Holy thing which shall be born of thee shall be called the Son of God" (Luke 1:35). Again, Brother Brown writes, "As proof to Mary that 'with God nothing shall be impossible' (Luke 1:37), Gabriel pointed her mind to the miracle touching her 'cousin Elizabeth, [who] hath also conceived a son in her old age' (Luke 1:36). With this news, Mary submitted herself to God's will. In words that reveal her premonition of future challenges, she uttered in reverential, almost convenantal tones, 'Behold the handmaid of the Lord; be it unto me according to thy word' (Luke 1:38)."[9]

Consider those words again in the context of the Christlike characteristic of faith. "Behold the handmaid of the Lord; be it unto me according to thy word." Consider how those words echo Christ's words to the Father in the great council in Heaven where He said, "Here am I, send me" (Abraham 3:27). And consider how those words contrast with those of Zacharias, Elisabeth's husband, when he heard the news that Elisabeth would conceive in her old age. Fear also fell upon Zacharias when Gabriel appeared to proclaim John's birth. And just as he had done with Mary, Gabriel sought to calm his fears by saying, "Fear not, Zacharias" (Luke 1:13). Gabriel then made this powerful announcement to him:

> Elisabeth shall bear thee a son, and thou shalt call his name John. And thou shalt have joy and gladness; and many shall rejoice at his birth. For he shall be great in the sight of the Lord, and shall drink neither wine nor strong drink; and he shall be filled with the Holy Ghost, even from his mother's womb. And many of the children of Israel shall he turn to the Lord their God. And he shall go before him in the spirit and power of Elias, to turn the hearts of the fathers to the children, and the disobedient to the wisdom of the just; to make ready a people prepared for the Lord. (Luke 1:13–17)

But despite these commanding words, Zacharias responded without faith and questioned doubtfully, "Whereby shall I know this? For I am an old man, and my wife well stricken in years" (Luke 1:18). And for his disbelief, Zacharias temporarily lost his speech and hearing and became both deaf and dumb. Gabriel reproved him by saying, "Behold, thou shalt be dumb, and not able to speak, unto the day that these things shall be performed, because thou believest not my words, which shall be fulfilled in their season" (Luke 1:20).

Elisabeth's reaction to the news of motherhood is not recorded in the scriptures, but Brother Brown concludes that:

> It is unlikely that Elisabeth expressed doubt. She must have been praying with faith for a child—to be a mother. Certainly, she was deeply concerned about her "reproach among men" because of her childlessness (Luke 1:25). It was her duty to bear children for her husband. But even more than the cold stares of others, she must have felt sorrow. She must have longed for a child to fill her empty arms—a child to care for, to love, and to cherish. And so she prayed. As proof of her earnest praying, she discloses a feeling of closeness to God in her words, "Thus hath the Lord dealt with me" (Luke 1:25) . . . [Elisabeth] seems to have readily accepted her unexpected good fortune both with humility and joy. She "hid herself five months" (Luke 1:24) . . . We perceive that Elisabeth was already seasoned and began preparing spiritually for the birth of her son as soon as the news came to her (see Luke 1:41-45). She was a responsive believer.[10]

Mary responded to her call to be the mother of Jesus by saying, "Behold the handmaid of the Lord, be it unto me according to thy will." Christ accepted his call from the Father with the response, "Here am I, send me," and Elisabeth, as described by Brother Brown, was a "responsive believer" when she was called to be the mother of John. Zacharias, on the other hand, responded with doubt and fear. How do we respond to the call to be mothers in these latter days? When our Church leaders plead with us to contemplate the importance of motherhood, do we react with faith? When they promise the personal assistance of the Lord to overcome impediments, do we believe? I urge you to do so. I entreat you to put aside your fear and your doubt and to take those first steps of faith, which are absolutely required to begin the miraculous journey of motherhood.

Strength

The second characteristic of Christ that we acquire as we faithfully embark on our journey of motherhood is strength. This characteristic is sometimes hard to discern because of the exhausting nature of motherhood. We feel so tired much of the time that we might describe ourselves as weak rather than strong, but it is through that very exertion that we become strong. I learned this early on in my experience as a young mother. I had three little boys in three and a half years, and saying that I felt tired most of the time, would be an understatement. At one point during that time, my mother-in-law came to visit, and she insisted on babysitting while my husband and I went to a BYU football game. That football season, there was a BYU cheerleader who could do back hand springs the entire length of the football field. I could never accomplish that particular feat now, but in my day, I was quite an athlete. My senior year in high school, I led my volleyball team to a second place finish in the state tournament. My basketball team took first place in state, and in track, I set a three hundred meter hurdle record that stood for over ten years. So that night, at that football game, as I watched this cheerleader's athleticism, I felt suddenly very sorry for myself. I slumped in my seat and thought, *There was a day when I could do things like that. Now, look at me.*

What happened next was one of those wonderful experiences with the spirit—when you not only feel the Spirit's words in your heart, but you also hear them in your ear; when you are enveloped by comfort and warmth so tangible, you know that the Spirit has reached out and touched you. This is what happened to me as I sat amongst the roar of 60,000 fans. Through the buzzing of stadium lights and the cracking of football helmets, through my own feelings of discouragement and doubt, the Spirit spoke quietly and peacefully, but proudly and profoundly to me: "You are developing a stamina of another kind."

All at once, all the sleepless nights I had experienced in the previous three and a half years, all the trips to the doctor's office for endless ear infections, all the energy exerted to chase after three active little boys, all at once, I saw all of these things in a different light. I saw them not as things that sapped me of my strength but as things that made me stronger. All at once, I discovered that the day after day sacrifice and service of motherhood is a medium for my own personal growth.

After this experience, I found that whenever I felt completely worn out or frustrated, whenever I became so tired that I felt like I couldn't even get out of bed let alone care for a growing family of small children, I found that if I turned to Heavenly Father for strength, I would always be blessed with the strength to keep going. More than this, however, I would be blessed with glimpses of the woman Heavenly Father knew I could become. In essence, I could see that my exhausting experiences as a mother were helping me to discover the strength of my own spirit.

Of these moments, I later wrote:

> *Why is it necessary to fall before you can rise? Why is it that before you can grow, you have to first be brought to your knees? I have so many memories of myself sinking to my knees and falling in tears onto the couch to bury my head in a pillow. If it weren't for the couch, I would have fallen further, and despite the couch, it always seemed like my spirit continued to sink. Tears falling, spirit sinking, lower and lower until I reached a new depth of sorrow and fatigue that I'd not experienced before. But there has not been a single one of those experiences where I didn't rise from the depths taller and stronger than ever. It seems to me that the human spirit must not adhere to the laws of gravity. Yes, it may fall at first when it is dropped, but unlike objects that are left to lie on the ground after falling from above, the human spirit has the ability to lift itself back up higher than it's ever been before. I believe this is because our spirit is being lifted by One who knows and understands the potential heights we have the power of rising to.*

The strength that comes from the service inherent in motherhood helps us to become the women we are meant to be as we turn to our Heavenly Father who knows better than each of us the strength of our spirits. To illustrate this further, let's look once more at Mary the mother of Jesus. Again, from *Mary and Elisabeth: Noble Daughters of God,* Brother Brown explains that "The angel Gabriel's annunciation to Mary of the coming birth of her Son is one of the most revered events in Christian history."[11]. Brother Brown continues:

> In virtually all cases, the first words of a divine messenger reveal the tenor of the message. In Mary's case, the angel said, "Hail, thou that art highly favoured, the Lord is with thee" (Luke 1:28). These words, and the following—"blessed art thou among women" (Luke 1:28)—carry a triple message. First, the angel was seeking to reassure Mary so that she would not be frightened. . . . Second, from the angel's words, we immediately sense that the eye of God had been watching Mary and had

approved the course of her life. Third, Gabriel's greeting strongly hints that Mary had also been an obedient daughter of God in her premortal life (see Luke 1:28, 30). Her current standing before God, as the angel intimates, continues a long history of nobleness.... He chose Mary because of her long history of righteousness, which reached far back into her premortal existence. Where do we find this source of evidence? First, the prophecies about Mary centuries before her birth tell us that she had been chosen to be the mother of God's Son long before her arrival on earth. Alma called her "precious and chosen" (Alma 7:10). Nephi was told that "the virgin whom thou seest is the mother of the son of God" (1 Ne. 11:18). The prophecies of King Benjamin, King Lamoni, and Isaiah declared the same kinds of tidings. If we study Nephi's vision it becomes clear that God had planned for a long time to entrust young Mary with His holy Son (see Ne. 11:20). This is no small matter. She was righteous and noble many hundred years before her birth.[12]

I believe that as women called to be mothers in these latter days that we were also righteous and noble long before our sojourn on this earth, and I believe that knowing this helps us to find the strength we need to press forward on our journey with faith. I also believe that this glimpse of who we are and of what our potential really is helps us to know where to turn when additional strength is needed. In order to give our children all that we can of who we are, we must turn to our own Heavenly Parent, because just as our children turn to us when they are in need, we, as children ourselves, must turn to our Heavenly Father, who is near, ready, and willing to strengthen us. Elder Jeffrey R. Holland received a letter from a mother who learned this principle. She writes:

> Through the thick and thin of this, and through the occasional tears of it all, I know deep down inside I am doing God's work. I know that in my motherhood I am in an eternal partnership with Him. I am deeply moved that God finds His ultimate purpose in being a parent.... It is this realization that I try to recall on those inevitable difficult days when all of this can be a bit overwhelming. Maybe it is precisely our inability and anxiousness that urge us to reach out to Him and enhance His ability to reach back to us. Maybe He secretly hopes that we will be anxious and will plead for His help. Then, I believe, He can teach these children directly, through us, but with no resistance offered. I like that idea. It gives me hope. If I can be right

before my Father in Heaven, perhaps His guidance to our children can be unimpeded. Maybe then it can be His work and His glory in a very literal sense.[13]

This concept of motherhood becoming Heavenly Father's work and glory as we enter into an eternal partnership with Him takes us a step beyond strength to the third characteristic of Christ we develop. That characteristic is submission.

Submission

To begin our discussion about submission, let's look at the opposite of submission: resistance. Our first baby was a boy—a very difficult boy. Now that my husband and I have had experiences with teenagers, we are confident in saying that this first son of ours was born a teenager. When he was not quite two, we welcomed another little boy into our home. While this second little son of ours came with a sweet disposition, he came with some struggles of his own. He was sickly and struggled growing. I had to nurse him round the clock for months, and because he had some digestive problems, I couldn't supplement his nutrition with formula or baby food. Dealing with a baby who required round the clock care and a terrible two-year-old with teenager tendencies was challenging, to say the least, but at the time, it was actually the least of my problems. During this time, I was also suffering from a severe case of postpartum depression. When I turned to Heavenly Father for help and answers, the impression I received was to have another baby. Well, you can imagine how I felt about that. I found myself in the predicament that I was in because of babies. I wasn't about to have another one, who in my mind, would only compound my problems, so I absolutely refused. This didn't stop the impressions, however; they kept coming, but I kept refusing.

Let's leave my story of resistance for just a minute and compare it to a similar story: the story of Jonah. This story is well known. Jonah was commanded by God to go and preach His gospel in Nineveh, but like me, Jonah refused. Instead, he boarded a ship for Tarshish and headed in the opposite direction of Nineveh. While on the boat, a storm began to rage. The sailors were afraid and wondered who had displeased the gods so much that such a storm would be sent to destroy them. Jonah admitted to them that the God of Israel was mad at him, and he said unto them, "Take me up, and cast me forth into the sea; so shall the sea be calm unto you: for I know that for my sake this great tempest is upon you" (Jonah 1:12). The sailors, however, were hesitant to cast Jonah into the sea to his death, so they continued to try to get the boat safely to shore. There efforts were to no avail because of the strength of the storm, so they cried unto the Lord, saying, "We beseech thee, O Lord, we beseech thee, let us not perish for this man's life, and lay not upon us innocent blood: for thou, O Lord, hast done as it pleased thee" (v. 14). This said, the sailors "took up Jonah, and cast him forth into the sea: and the sea ceased from her raging" (v. 15).

At this point in the story, the sailors were safe, but remember, Jonah is drowning in the sea. Traditionally, most of us think of this story and visualize a great fish immediately scooping up Jonah, Jonah repenting in the fish's belly, and then being spit out onto dry land. But looking more carefully at the scriptural account, Jonah himself tells us that his repentance came while he was drowning in the depths of the sea and that he offered this prayer of gratitude to God when he was safely in the fish's belly:

> I cried by reason of mine affliction unto the Lord, and he heard me; out of the belly of hell cried I, and thou heardest my voice.
>
> For thou hadst cast me into the deep, in the midst of the seas; and the floods compassed me about: all thy billows and thy waves passed over me.
>
> Then I said, I am cast out of thy sight; yet I will look again toward thy holy temple.
>
> The waters compassed me about, even to the soul: the depth closed me round about, the weeds were wrapped about my head.
>
> I went down to the bottoms of the mountains; the earth with her bars was about me forever: yet hast thou brought up my life from corruption, O Lord my God.
>
> When my soul fainteth within me I remembered the Lord: and my prayer came in unto thee, into thine holy temple.
>
> They that observe lying vanities forsake their own mercy.
>
> But I will sacrifice unto thee with the voice of thanksgiving; I will pay that that I have vowed. Salvation is of the Lord (Jonah 2:2–9).

Following that prayer of thanksgiving, "The Lord spake unto the fish, and it vomited out Jonah upon the dry land" (v. 10). And "Jonah arose, and went unto Nineveh, according to the word of the Lord" (Jonah 3:3).

In summary, Jonah's failure to submit himself to God nearly cost his life. Jonah was given a commandment. He went to great lengths to resist that commandment. When it became frighteningly clear that the consequence of resistance was far worse than his fears of submission, Jonah learned powerfully that "they that observe lying vanities forsake their own mercy" (Jonah 2:8). It is the same powerful lesson that I learned as I resisted my impressions to have a third child. So let's return to my story.

Just as the sailors in Jonah's story feared for their own lives because of Jonah's unwillingness to submit, I believe that my own family, especially my husband, worried about our well-being because of my unwillingness to submit. Our home was, indeed, tempest tossed due to the consequences of my resistance. Education Week approached that year, and my husband must have seen it as a safe haven whereby he could "toss me out of the ship" without worrying about any innocent blood being "layed upon his head." He took a week off, drove me up to the Marriot Center, and dumped me out onto the sidewalk. I later recorded in my journal this song of gratitude for the experience I had in the belly of the Marriot Center:

> *My hope for Education Week was that it might pull me out of the rut that I've been in. It wasn't a formal prayer. Only a small dim hope because I'd practically given up on prayers. Fortunately, my Heavenly Father had not given up on me, because despite the fact that I did not ask, He gave to me unceasingly. I know his love for me—it overwhelmed me to the point of joyous disbelief. I know that great blessings will come into my life as I follow the promptings I've received to have another baby. I've been fighting these promptings for some time, and I know that this is why I have been so miserable. I've pushed the Spirit out of my heart, and I've allowed Satan to make his way in. But this week after finally saying, "Yes, I'll do it!" I allowed the Spirit to enter back into my heart, and I'm filled with the most amazing peace and happiness. This has been such a learning and growing experience for me, and I'm so grateful to my Heavenly Father for loving me enough to say, "Come Unto Me" until I came.*

Submission—the Bible Dictionary defines it with words such as humility, obedience, subjection, and yielding, and interestingly enough, also with the phrases duties of family and duties of children. We live in a world that tells us our first duty should be to ourselves, and if we observe these "lying vanities," as I found out, we "forsake our own mercy." Another parable from James E. Talmage, "The Parable of the Unwise Bee," illustrates this further.

When Elder Talmage required quiet seclusion, he would go to a favorite retreat in an upper room of a tower in a large building. In that room, he spent many peaceful and busy hours with books and pens. He was not without visitors, however; for when he would open the windows of the room, flying insects would enter and share the space with him. He welcomed these self-invited guests and would often put down his pen and watch with interest the activities of the winged visitors. Once, a wild bee flew into the room, and of this visitor, Elder Talmage wrote:

> The little creature realized that it was a prisoner, yet all its efforts to find the exit through the partly opened casement failed. When ready to close up the room and leave, I threw the window wide and tried at first to guide and then to drive the bee to liberty and safety, knowing well that if left in the room it would die as other insects there entrapped had perished in the dry atmosphere of the enclosure. The more I tried to drive it out, the more determinedly did it oppose and resist my efforts. Its erstwhile peaceful hum developed into an angry roar; its daring flight became hostile and threatening.
>
> Then it caught me off my guard and stung my hand—the hand that would have guided it to freedom. At last it alighted on a pendant attached to the ceiling, beyond my reach of help or injury. The sharp pain of its unkind sting aroused in me rather pity than anger. I knew the inevitable penalty of its mistaken opposition and defiance, and I had to leave the creature to its fate. Three days later I returned to the room and found the dried, lifeless body of the bee on the writing table. It had paid for its stubbornness with its life.
>
> ... Are we so much wiser than the bee? ... We are prone to contend, sometimes with vehemence and anger, against the adversity which after all may be the manifestation of a superior wisdom and loving care, directed against our temporary comfort for our permanent blessing. To many, [difficulty may be] a providential means of

leading or driving them from the confines of selfish indulgence to the sunshine and the open, where boundless opportunity waits on effort. Disappointment, sorrow, and affliction may be the expression of an all-wise Father's kindness.

Consider the lesson of the unwise bee!

"Trust in the Lord with all thine heart; and lean not unto thine own understanding. In all thy ways acknowledge him, and he shall direct thy paths" (Proverbs 3:5-6).[14]

We find in Elisabeth an ideal example of submissiveness and trust. Again, Brother Brown, teaches us that, "her very name derives from a Hebrew expression which means, '[my] God is the one by whom to swear' or '[my] God is good fortune.' Thus, in the words of Barbara Reid, 'Elizabeth's name declares that she is a woman who depends utterly on God and who is filled to satisfaction by Him'. . . . How fitting it is that Elisabeth lived up to her name."[15]

Brown compares Elisabeth, the mother of John, to Hannah, the mother of the prophet Samuel. Hannah too was childless. Both Elisabeth and Hannah, in the eyes of others, lived under a curse from God. With both women, God intervened in a miraculous manner. Both John and Samuel came as children of promise and both fulfilled important prophetic roles. Of John, the scriptures say, "the child grew, and waxed strong in spirit" (Luke 1:80), and of Samuel, it is recorded, "Samuel grew, and the Lord was with him" (1 Samuel 3:19). Regarding these similarities in submissiveness, Brown writes: "What does all of this mean—barren women, women healed by God, miraculous births, children of promise? On one level, it means that God does not forget any of His children, including those who, in the eyes of others, have been forsaken by Him. On another level, the experiences of these women demonstrate that God brings good things into the lives of the faithful"[16]

Jonah's eventual submission taught him to "sacrifice unto [the Lord] with a voice of thanksgiving." My submission brought me to a knowledge of God's love to the point of joyous disbelief. And from Elisabeth whose very name means "My God is good fortune," we learn that blessings come into the lives of those who submit themselves to our Heavenly Father's will. It is both humbling and compelling to learn that one of these blessings is the fourth characteristic of Christ: Hope.

Hope

Just as strength is developed as we exercise faith, hope comes to us as we humbly submit. I have been blessed with two very poignant experiences that illumined my path with hope. The first experience happened with my fifth child, Seth. When he was four years old, I wrote him this letter, explaining the experience.

> *Whew! Where do I begin? You are four years old now, and we are awaiting the arrival of your new baby brother, Micah. He's almost a week overdue, and we are all impatient, but I am a little nervous because I don't think I can handle another baby like you! It is safe to say, Seth, that you have been the biggest challenge of my life. But don't dismay by that statement. Biggest challenges often turn into biggest blessings, and that is just what you've become!*
>
> *When you were a baby, you were the screamingest baby that ever was born. You screamed and fussed for ten solid months—night and day—nobody ever got any rest.*
>
> *Of course, you had countless ear infections and two surgeries for tubes during those first ten months which contributed to your distress, but even when the tubes stopped the ear infections, you continued to be fussy and ill content. You did start to sleep, however; and that is one of the things that saved me.*
>
> *You see, there was a time during those first ten months when I didn't think I could go on taking care of you. Just imagine, ten months of day after day screaming and night after night walking the floors and getting no sleep. I spent a lot of time crying right along with you until one morning, Daddy came down to check on us. I SNAPPED! I started crying hysterically. I handed you off to Daddy, grabbed the keys to the van, and in the middle of February dressed only in my robe, drove away from home.*
>
> *Fortunately, I ended up driving to the temple where I found myself praying through tears. I told Heavenly Father that I couldn't go on and that he needed to make you a good baby. I remember pleading, "Make it stop! Make it stop!" But that wasn't to be. Instead, sitting there in the frosty van*

in front of the temple, the Spirit whispered so sweetly, "I have a plan for you." That was all it took—six little words—to give me the ability to face more days of crying and more nights of no sleep. Because in those six little words, "I have a plan for you," I knew that Heavenly Father was mindful of me. I knew that He loved me, and I knew that there was a purpose for the experiences I was having with you.

Later, I read a quote from President Harold B. Lee that helped me to see what this experience had brought to me, "Anyone who has a testimony . . . has enjoyed the gift of prophecy, he's had the Spirit of revelation . . . all the other seeming difficulties melt away like heavy frost before the coming of the rising sun."[17] That is what happened to me that cold morning in February. Through the whisperings of the Spirit, all my difficulties melted away, and I was left basking in the light of hope.

I was blessed with this same melting away of difficulties during one long and exhausting summer—this time, with seven children. Any summer with seven children is exhausting, but this particular summer seemed fraught with other setbacks. My husband had a grand mal seizure at the beginning of the summer, and though his prognosis was good, he was weak and unable to drive for most of that time. Towards the middle of the summer, my oldest son came home from a trip with a peculiar, long lasting, and particularly brutal illness that he proceeded to spread to the rest of the children. It took seven full weeks to nurse all seven children back to health. The illness took a tremendous toll on my two little ones who were 10 months and 2 at the time. With there defenses down, they came down with roseola immediately following the first illness, and it took another three weeks to help them recuperate from that. By the end of the summer, I was so worn out and exhausted that I was ready to quit my job as a mother.

I was sitting in Sunday School feeling completely spent when the teacher had us turn to Doctrine and Covenants 106. This section is a revelation given through Joseph Smith to Warren A. Cowdery, an older brother of Oliver Cowdery. In the revelation, Warren is called as a local presiding officer, but I read it that day with my name replacing Warren's and with my call as a mother replacing his call as a presiding high priest. Through the eyes of the Spirit, this is what I read:

> It is my will that my servant [Katie Van Dyke] should be appointed and ordained a [mother over her children] in the land of Freedom . . .; And should preach my everlasting gospel, and lift up [her] voice and [teach her children] . . . And devote [her] whole time to this high and holy calling, which I now give unto [her], seeking diligently the kingdom of heaven and its righteousness, and all things necessary shall be added thereunto; for the laborer is worthy of [her] hire. And again, verily I say unto you, the coming of the Lord draweth nigh, and it overtaketh the world as a thief in the night—therefore, gird up your loins, that you may be the children of light, and that day shall not overtake you as a thief. And again, verily I say unto you, there was joy in heaven when my servant, [Katie], bowed to my scepter, and separated [herself] from the crafts of men; Therefore, blessed is my servant [Katie], for I will have mercy on [her]; . . . And I will give [her] grace and assurance wherewith [she] may stand; and if [she] continue to be a faithful witness and a light unto the church I have prepared a crown for [her] in the mansions of my Father, Even so, Amen. (see D&C 106:1–8)

Again, I had been blessed with the "gift of prophecy" and the "Spirit of revelation" where "all [my] seeming difficulties [melted] away like heavy frost before the coming of the rising sun." Despair was replaced with hope. Confusion and darkness were overtaken by light. My path became brighter, my purpose as a mother clear. As Elder Maxwell once wrote, "As other lights flicker and fade, the light of the gospel will burn ever more brightly in a darkening world, guiding the humble but irritating the guilty and those who prefer the dusk of decadence."[18]

Another parable from Elder Talmage illuminates this point brilliantly. It is called, "The Parable of the Two Lamps":

> Among the material things of the past—things that I treasure for sweet memory's sake and because of pleasant association in bygone days—is a lamp. . . . The lamp of which I speak, the student lamp of my school and college days, was one of the best of its kind. I had bought it with hard-earned savings; it was counted among my most cherished possessions. . . .
>
> One summer evening I sat musing studiously and withal restfully in the open air outside the door of the room in which I lodged and studied. A stranger approached. I noticed that he carried a satchel. He

was affable and entertaining. I brought a chair from within, and we chatted together till the twilight had deepened into dusk, the dusk into darkness.

Then he said: "You are a student and doubtless have much work to do of nights. What kind of lamp do you use?" And without waiting for a reply, he continued, "I have a superior kind of lamp I should like to show you, a lamp designed and constructed according to the latest achievements of applied science, far surpassing anything heretofore produced as a means of artificial lighting."

I replied with confidence, and I confess, not without some exultation: "My friend, I have a lamp, one that has been tested and proved. It has been to me a companion through many a long night. It is an Argand lamp, and one of the best. I have trimmed and cleaned it today. It is ready for the lighting. Step inside; I will show you my lamp; then you may tell me whether yours can possibly be better.

We entered the room . . . and I put the match to my well-trimmed Argand.

My visitor was voluble in his praise. It was the best lamp of its kind, he said. He averred that he had never seen a lamp in better trim. He turned the wick up and down and pronounced the adjustment perfect. He declared that never before had he realized how satisfactory a student lamp could be.

I liked the man. He seemed to me wise, and he assuredly was ingratiating. "Love me, love my lamp," I thought, mentally paraphrasing a common expression of the period.

"Now," he said, "with your permission, I'll light my lamp." He took from his satchel a lamp then known as the "Rochester." It had a chimney which, compared with mine, was as a factory smokestack alongside a house flue. Its hollow wick was wide enough to admit my four fingers. Its light made bright the remotest corner of my room. In its brilliant blaze, my own little Argand wick burned a weak, pale yellow. Until that moment of convincing demonstration, I had never known the dim obscurity in which I had lived and labored, studied and struggled.

"I'll buy your lamp," said I. "You need neither explain nor argue further. . ." Now consider the application of [the story] . . . The man who would sell me a lamp did not disparage mine. He placed his greater light alongside my feebler flame, and I hasted to obtain the better.[19]

Just as Elder Talmage teaches of obtaining greater light in this parable, my two experiences with hope did the same for me. In each situation, hope provided greater light and clarity, and the light of motherhood brightened into a "brilliant blaze." Doctrine and Covenants 50:24 teaches us the same principle. It reads, "That which is of God is light; and he that continueth in light, receiveth more light; and that light groweth brighter and brighter until the perfect day."

And that is what hope does for us along our journey of motherhood. As we press forward with faith, receiving strength, and submitting ourselves to our Heavenly Father's will, hope comes to light our way more clearly. We begin to see that our chosen path is correct and that we are capable of serving and sacrificing for the children who have been put in our charge. And that increased ability to serve and sacrifice for our children helps us to develop charity, the 5th characteristic of Christ.

Charity

> And Charity suffereth long, and is kind, and envieth not, and is not puffed up, seeketh not her own, is not easily provoked, thinketh no evil, rejoiceth not in iniquity but rejoiceth in truth, beareth all things, believeth all things, hopeth all things, endureth all things.
>
> Wherefore, my beloved brethren, if ye have not charity, ye are nothing, for charity never faileth. Wherefore, cleave unto charity which is the greatest of all, for all things must fail—
>
> But charity is the pure love of Christ, and it endureth forever; and whoso is found possessed of it at the last day, it shall be well with him. (Moroni 7:45–47)

These are powerful words from Moroni. They tell us what we should be seeking while here on earth. Consider them with regards to our journey of motherhood—with regards to faith, strength, submission, and hope. We've looked at examples of longsuffering and kindness. We've learned that mothers "seeketh not their own," but rather, they seek the will of our Heavenly Father and the well-being of their children. We've rejoiced in truth. We've listened to experiences and stories of bearing all things, believing all things, hoping all things, and enduring all things. Motherhood, therefore, is definitely one of the means by which we can acquire charity: "the pure love of Christ [which] endureth forever; and whoso is found possessed of . . . it shall be well with them."

Is it any wonder, then, that Gordon B. Hinckley declared, "Women for the most part see their greatest fulfillment, their greatest happiness in home and family. God planted within women something divine that expresses itself in quiet strength, in refinement, in peace, in goodness, in virtue, in truth, in love. And all of these remarkable qualities find their truest and most satisfying expression in motherhood."[20] Consider these qualities as we look at the examples of charity set by Mary and Elisabeth.

> When Mary comes to visit Elisabeth in her home, we learn even more about Elisabeth's noble, selfless character. . . . Christian art portrays the meeting of these two women as a tender moment in which Elisabeth recognizes the role and importance of her young cousin who is to become the mother of the Son of God. Scripture confirms this view. What is most striking is Elisabeth's evident lack of jealousy. Many individuals become envious of a privilege or honor that comes to another, especially if the other person is younger. But not Elisabeth. She was a person who did not seek special status for herself. Instead, as a gracious hostess, she put the younger woman at the center of attention by saying, "Blessed art thou among women, and blessed is the fruit of thy womb" (Luke 1:42). In fact, Elisabeth's only statement in this scene that touches on her own condition was her reference to her child, "the babe" who "leaped in my womb for joy" (Luke 1:44). Otherwise, Elisabeth's focus rested entirely on Mary. . . . From this, it is clear that Elisabeth was a person without guile, a person with Christlike love, a person who in her own life put the interests of others first, including those of her newly pregnant, unmarried young cousin. The command which Mary felt in the angel's words about visiting Elisabeth (see Luke 1:36) was meant to send her to the one person whom God had prepared to assist her to surmount the challenges and fears during the first days and weeks following the angel's announcement. Elisabeth was that person.[21]

But Mary was not the only recipient of Elisabeth's charity. Elisabeth's son, John, the forerunner and friend of Christ, was blessed by her charity as well:

> It was Elisabeth who first received a divine testimony about the coming Messiah when Mary came to visit (see Luke 1:42–43). She would have shared her testimony with John. When? Maybe when she held him close to her heart, whispering her love and telling him of his

divine role. Maybe when clasping his little hand and taking a walk, showing him the beauty of God's creations. Maybe when explaining about God's miracles after he asked where his brothers and sisters were—telling him that he was her little miracle. Elisabeth must have poured her testimony of God's goodness and greatness into her son's heart as she lovingly raised the man who would one day baptize the Savior and proclaim His divinity. . . . She was a mother who raised her son to delight in the Lord.[22]

And as Mary was nurtured and tutored by her generous and righteous older cousin, Mary also acquired these attributes of charity which would have blessed her son, even Jesus Christ. Listen to what Brother Brown has to say about the charity Mary offered Jesus at the time of His greatest suffering:

> After witnessing her Son's suffering, Mary's distress must have been unbearable, as Simeon had foreseen long ago. For on the occasion of Mary bringing the infant Jesus to the temple, the aged Simeon had prophesied to Mary that "a sword shall pierce through thy own soul" (Luke 2:35), an evident reference to Mary witnessing Jesus' horrible crucifixion. At this moment of supreme suffering, Jesus reached out with words to the one who had given Him life, who had loved Him as only a mother could, and whom He adored above all others. We sense that His words to Mary, "Woman, behold thy son," were His appeal to her to look on Him, her Son. His words seem to plead with her to watch Him in the last moments of His life and, finally, to watch Him die. He would not die alone. Mary's love for Him gave her enough strength to look upon Him in His agony and to remain with Him until the end. Mary, who had given birth to Him, raised Him, cared for Him, and loved Him with a mother's love, would not let Him die alone. At this intense moment, she became a witness of His death as she had been a witness of His birth. Jesus' life, from beginning to end, had been played out in the view of His mother.[23]

Mary's powerful mothering poignantly illuminates the masterpiece that is motherhood. If even Christ relied so wholly on His mother in His greatest need, how much more do our mortal children need us "to have their lives played out before our view?" And do you see where we have come on our journey? Beginning with faith and a somewhat hesitant step into the darkness, we have had light added upon that path through strength, submission, hope, and charity, until we see clearly the power of motherhood and the importance of our journey. We have ascended to our sixth and final characteristic of Christ, which is discernment.

Discernment

Elder David A. Bednar says this of discernment,

> The spiritual gift of discernment . . . is a light of protection and direction in a world that grows increasingly dark . . . discernment is so much more than recognizing right from wrong. It helps us to distinguish the relevant from the irrelevant, the important from the unimportant, and the necessary from that which is merely nice. The gift of discernment opens vistas that stretch far beyond what can be seen with natural eyes or hear with natural ears. Discernment is seeing with spiritual eyes and feeling with the heart. . . . Discerning is hearing with spiritual ears and feeling with the heart . . discerning also enables us to assist others who are seeking to obtain the path and who desire to press forward with steadfastness in Christ. Blessed with these spiritual gifts, we will not lose our way; we will not wander off; we will not be lost.[24]

With the Christlike characteristic of discernment, we are no longer walking in darkness. Our path is illuminated clearly. But more than that, we can, as Elder Bednar stated, see vistas with our spiritual eyes, not only for ourselves, but for our children as well. Again, we turn to Elisabeth's example of discernment.

The angel Gabriel's announcement to Zacharias that Elisabeth would bear a son set in motion a series of spiritual events that would take place in Elisabeth's home. In fact, the number of spiritual manifestations that occur in her home are astonishing. First, was Elisabeth's conception of John (see Luke 1:24). This is followed by the exchange between Mary and Elisabeth, where Elisabeth prophesied that Mary's child would be the Messiah (see Luke 1:40–55). Third, John's circumcision was sacred because it was performed in obedience to divine command received by Abraham (see Gen. 17:10–12). Yet another miracle occurred during the naming of John. Family members thought Elisabeth and Zacharias would name their son after his father, but when they tried to name him Zacharias, Elisabeth stopped them, insisting his name be John. Zacharias resolved the issue by writing that the child would, indeed, be named John. As soon as he did this, the curse against his speech and hearing was miraculously lifted (see Luke 1:64). Of all these miracles, Brother Brown writes:

> In light of all these events, and perhaps others that may have gone unrecorded, it is apparent that within less than a year, the home of Elisabeth and Zacharias became an especially sacred place where the Spirit of God could inspire and nurture those within it. In effect, the miracle of the angel's appearance in the temple followed Zacharias home so that the home which he and Elisabeth shared became a spiritual powerhouse for those who lived there and came to visit. In a way, their home had become as sacred as the temple where the series of miracles began.[25]

I want my home, like Elisabeth's, to be a "spiritual powerhouse." I want it to be as sacred as the temple for those I care about and for those who live with me. And that is the ultimate destination where our journey of motherhood takes us. That is the essence of what the Exhilarating Exhaustion of Motherhood is. It is not just believing; it goes far beyond hoping; it is knowing that all the effort you put forth in behalf of your family, all the sleepless nights, all the endless trips to the doctor's office, all the meals, all the work, and even all the tears have meaning and purpose. The Exhilarating Exhaustion of Motherhood is seeing with your spiritual eyes that the service and sacrifice you give your children is sanctifying your home, sanctifying the people who live in your home, and sanctifying *you*. It is energy well worth exerting.

I like to compare the energies of motherhood to that of Michelangelo as he created his David masterpiece. Michelangelo was struggling to decide how to portray David in the marble sculpture he would create. In Irving Stone's *The Agony and the Ecstasy*, we read about Michelangelo's decision:

> What could he find in David triumphant, he asked himself, worthy of sculpturing. Tradition portrayed him after the fact. Yet David after the battle was an anticlimax, his great moment already gone. Which, then, was the important David? When did David become a giant? After killing Goliath, or at the moment he decided that he must try. David, as he was releasing with brilliant and deadly accuracy the shot from the sling; or David before he entered the battle when he decided that the Israelites must be freed from the vassalage to the Philistines. . . . It was David's decision that made him a giant, not his killing of Goliath. This was the David he had been seeking, caught at the exultant height of resolution.[26]

Of this decision, Ardeth Green Kapp writes, "It was in realizing the importance of David's hard choice and his faith to act that the door was unlocked, allowing Michelangelo to decide about his own mission in marble. Recognizing David as the giant at the moment of his decision allowed Michelangelo to make his decision; and the choice having been made, his tempo changed and with it came strength, power, and hidden energies."[27]

The Agony and the Ecstasy continues: "He soared, he drew with authority and power, he molded in clay . . . his fingers unable to keep pace with his thoughts and emotions, and with astonishing facility he knew where the David lay. The limitations of the block began to appear as assets, forcing his mind into a simplicity of design that might never have occurred to him had it been whole and perfect. The marble came alive now."[28]

Sisters, motherhood will come alive to us as we come to see that as mothers we can truly be giants. The world tries to take mothers and turn us into dwarves. But as we focus on the truth about motherhood, as we see with our spiritual eyes the miracles that can come into the lives of our families as we serve and sacrifice for them, as the vistas of spiritual blessings and productivity are opened up to us, we will, as Ardeth Green Kapp writes, "[be] driven by an exhilaration that causes us to hunger and thirst and feel new energies that lift us, like Michelangelo, toward our goal."[29]

Embark on the exhilarating though exhausting journey of motherhood. Even if your first steps are taken with faltering faith, you will be blessed with strength to continue. Through submission, you will find direction. Hope will bring with it greater light that will lead you to charity and discernment where you will find clarity of purpose. And with that clarity of purpose, you will find the hidden energies required to further sanctify your homes, your children, and yourselves!

Notes

1. Boyd K. Packer, *Memorable Stories with a Message* (Salt Lake City: Deseret Book, 2000), 33.
2. James E. Talmage, "Three Parables: The Unwise Bee, the Owl Express, and Two Lamps," *Ensign,* Feb. 2003, 11–12.

3. Ibid.
4. *Discourses of President Gordon B. Hinckley,* vol. 1, (Salt Lake City: The Church of Jesus Christ of Latter-day Saints, 2004), 125.
5. Ibid., vol. 2, 38.
6. Thomas S. Monson, "Behold Thy Mother," *Ensign,* Apr. 1998, 2).
7. Brown, *Mary and Elisabeth: Noble Daughters of God* (Salt Lake City: UT, Deseret Book, 2002, 45).
8. Ibid.
9. Ibid., 46.
10. Ibid., 23.
11. Brown, *Mary and Elisabeth: Noble Daughters of God,* 43.
12. Ibid., 43–44.
13. Jeffrey R. Holland, "Because She is a Mother," *Ensign,* May 1997, 36.
14. Talmage, "Three Parables: The Unwise Bee, the Owl Express, and Two Lamps," 8–9.
15. Brown, *Mary and Elisabeth: Noble Daughters of God,* 26.
16. Ibid. 25–26.
17. *Teachings of Presidents of the Church: Harold B. Lee* (Salt Lake City: The Church of Jesus Christ of Latter-day Saints, 2000), 37.
18. Neal A. Maxwell, *Church News,* Jan. 5, 1970, 28.
19. Talmage, "Three Parables: The Unwise Bee, the Owl Express, and Two Lamps," 12–13.
20. Gordon B. Hinckley, *Teachings of Gordon B. Hinckley* (Salt Lake City: The Church of Jesus Christ of Latter-day Saints, 1997), 387.
21. Brown, *Mary and Elisabeth: Noble Daughters of God,* 27–28.
22. Ibid., 33.
23. Ibid., 76.
24. David A. Bednar, "Quick to Observe," *BYU Magazine,* Fall 2005, 63).
25. Brown, *Mary and Elisabeth: Noble Daughters of God,* 29–31.
26. Irving Stone, *The Agony and the Ecstasy* (New York: Doubleday and Company, 1961), 388.
27. Ardeth Green Kapp, "Drifting, Dreaming, Directing," *Woman to Woman: Selected Talks from the BYU Women's Conference* (Salt Lake City: Deseret Book, 1986), 52.
28. Irving Stone, *The Agony and the Ecstasy (*New York: Doubleday and Company, 1961), 388.
29. Kapp, "Drifting, Dreaming, Directing," 52.

4
The Normal Chaos of Motherhood

I vividly remember preparing for the birth of our first child. I was so excited, and so was everyone around me. I felt as though having a baby was the most wonderful thing that could ever happen to me, and all the comments I received from others seemed to validate that feeling. Once our baby was born and he was home from the hospital, the comments and feelings of others seemed unchanged. They approached me and my new baby with the same sense of wonder and excitement they had before. The only problem was that I was exhausted and weary in a way that I had never experienced. My dream of rocking a newborn baby into blissful contentment and then putting him to sleep in his well-decorated crib had been replaced with a lot of crying, confusion, and colic. While those around me continued to express an assumption of bliss, my frustration grew as I wondered what I was doing wrong. And I was afraid to be honest about my feelings because I worried that others would think less of me for not being able to handle a small baby with more ease and authority. Then Elder Jeffrey R. Holland gave his memorable and moving talk to young mothers entitled, "Because She Is a Mother." In it, he said:

> The work of a mother is hard, too often unheralded work. The young years are often those when either husband or wife—or both—may still be in school or in those earliest and leanest stages of developing the husband's breadwinning capacities. Finances fluctuate daily between low and nonexistent. The apartment is usually decorated in one of two

smart designs—Desert Industries provincial or early Mother Hubbard. The car, if there is one, runs on smooth tires and an empty tank. But with night feedings and night teethings, often the greatest challenge of all for a young mother is simply fatigue. Through these years, mothers go longer on less sleep and give more to others with less personal renewal for themselves than any other group I know at any other time in life. It is not surprising when the shadows under their eyes sometimes vaguely resemble the state of Rhode Island. . . . One young mother wrote to me recently that her anxiety tended to come on three fronts. One was that whenever she heard talks on LDS motherhood, she worried because she felt she didn't measure up or somehow wasn't going to be equal to the task. Secondly, she felt like the world expected her to teach her children reading, writing, interior design, Latin, calculus, and the Internet—all before the baby said something terribly ordinary, like "goo goo." Thirdly, she often felt people were sometimes patronizing, almost always without meaning to be, because the advice she got or even the compliments she received seemed to reflect nothing of the mental investment, the spiritual and emotional exertion, the long-night, long-day, stretched-to-the-limit demands that sometimes are required in trying to be and wanting to be the mother God hopes she will be.[1]

As Elder Holland spoke, I felt so validated. I remember thinking, "An apostle of the Lord knows how I feel. And if an apostle of the Lord knows how I feel, then Heavenly Father knows how I feel, too. And if Heavenly Father knows how I feel, then He knows how other young mothers feel. And if He knows how other young mothers feel, then other young mothers feel the same as me."

I wanted to stand up and cheer. "There is nothing wrong with me. What I'm feeling as a young mother is normal. And I bet," I remember thinking, "that the reservations I fear about disclosing my feelings are normal, too. But," I concluded, "if I open up to others, I'm sure they will do the same."

From that day on, I commenced discussing motherhood with a fearless honesty that was at first surprising to others, but ultimately refreshing and relieving. Other mothers did indeed open up to me and thanked me for being honest with them. And together, we have discovered that a great deal of the chaos that comes into mothers lives is normal. More than normal, however, it is essential, because the chaos and struggles that are inherent in motherhood are the very things that turn us to Christ. Elder Holland explains:

> When you have come to the Lord in meekness and lowliness of heart and, as one mother said, "pounded on the doors of heaven to ask for, to plead for, to demand guidance and wisdom and help for this wondrous task," that door is thrown open to provide you the influence and the help of all eternity. Claim the promises of the Savior of the world. Ask for the healing balm of the Atonement for whatever may be troubling you or your children. Know that in faith things will be made right in spite of you, or more correctly, because of you.[2]

That is what I hope we will discover in this chapter. That we are progressing along the path towards perfection, not despite the Normal Chaos of Motherhood, but because of it! To aid in our discovery, we need to cast off our incorrect perceptions of perfection and look at the concept of perfection in a new light. We will do this by taking each letter in the word *perfect* and highlighting a concept that leads us to greater understanding of what being perfect actually means. As we do this, I believe we will find that the Normal Chaos of Motherhood is not a stumbling block on our road to perfection. Rather, it is absolutely essential. More than that, I believe that the Normal Chaos of Motherhood is evidence that we are walking steadfastly on the path that Christ prepared for us.

P = Progress

During the 1995 October General Conference, Elder Russell M. Nelson gave a talk entitled "Perfection Pending." In it, he surmised:

> If I were to ask which of the Lord's commandments is most difficult to keep, many of us might cite Matthew 5:48, "Be ye therefore perfect, even as your Father which is in heaven is perfect." Keeping this commandment can be a concern because each of us is far from perfect, both spiritually and temporally. . . when comparing one's performance with the supreme standard of the Lord's expectation, the reality of imperfection can at times be depressing. My heart goes out to conscientious Saints who, because of their shortcomings, allow feelings of depression to rob them of happiness in life. We all need to remember: men are that they might have joy—not guilt trips! We also need to remember that the Lord gives no commandments that are impossible to obey. But sometimes we fail to comprehend them fully.[3]

Here, Elder Nelson confirms the idea that our perceptions of perfection may be imperfect. He agrees that being perfect may be a misunderstood commandment. To clarify, Elder Nelson continues:

> The moment [Jesus] uttered the words, "[Be ye therefore perfect], even as your Father which is in heaven is perfect," he raised our sights beyond the bounds of mortality. Our Heavenly Father has eternal perfection. This very fact merits a much broader perspective. Recently I studied the English and Greek editions of the New Testament, concentrating on each use of the term *perfect* and its derivatives. Studying both languages together provided some interesting insights, since Greek was the original language of the New Testament.
>
> In Matthew 5:48, the term *perfect* was translated from the Greek teleios, which means "complete." *Teleios* is an adjective derived from the noun *telos*, which means "end." The infinitive form of the verb is *teleiono*, which means "to reach a distant end, to be fully developed, to consummate, or to finish." Please note that the word does not imply "freedom from error," it implies "achieving a distant objective." In fact, when writers of the Greek New Testament wished to describe perfection of behavior—precision or excellence of human effort—they did not employ a form of *teleios*; instead, they chose different words.
>
> *Teleios* is not a total stranger to us. From it comes the prefix *tele*- that we use every day. *Telephone* literally means "distant talk." *Television* means "to see distantly." *Telephoto* means "distant light," and so on.
>
> With that background in mind, let us consider another highly significant statement made by the Lord. Just prior to his crucifixion, he said that on "the third day I shall be perfected." Think of that? The sinless, errorless Lord—already perfect by our mortal standards—proclaimed his own state of perfection yet to be in the future . . . the Atonement of Christ fulfilled the long-awaited purpose for which he had come to the earth. His concluding words upon Calvary's cross referred to the culmination of his assignment—to atone for all humankind. Then he said, "It is finished." Not surprisingly, the Greek word from which *finished* was derived is *teleios*.
>
> That Jesus attained eternal perfection following his resurrection is confirmed in the Book of Mormon. It records the visit of the resurrected Lord to the people of ancient America. There he repeated the important injunction previously cited but with one very significant addition. He said "I would that ye should be perfect *even as I*, or your Father who is in heaven is perfect" (3 Nephi 12:48).[4]

The type of perfection outlined by Elder Nelson is the type of perfection we will be focusing on in this chapter. From Elder Nelson we learn that we should not focus on mortal standards of perfection that imply "freedom from error." Rather, our focus should be eternal perfection where we are focused on "reaching that distant end" where our families can live forever in our Heavenly Father's presence.

E = Eyes

As we focus on eternal perfection, we must also view ourselves with spiritual eyes. Seeing ourselves with spiritual eyes essentially means believing in ourselves as daughters of God who, as mothers, have the capacity and power to build His kingdom in miraculous ways. The adversary's lies about mothers and motherhood are rampant, powerful, persuasive, and blinding! These lies can weigh us down and distort our vision with doubt and uncertainty. On this subject, President Ezra Taft Benson taught: "As the showdown between good and evil approaches with its accompanying trials and tribulations, Satan is increasingly striving to overcome the Saints with despair, discouragement, despondency, and depression."[5]

In response to this, Elder David S. Baxter of the Seventy writes: "The adversary knows that if he can prevent us from recognizing our divine potential, he will have scored a major victory. Whatever the source, such feelings of personal inadequacy can prove debilitating. If we allow them to persist, the weight of the world will press down on us, and we will be held back from achieving our potential. By extension, the lives of those we love will also be affected—lives that otherwise would have been touched for good if we had felt positively about ourselves.[6]

From this, we may conclude that seeing ourselves with spiritual eyes is a necessity for ourselves as well as for our children. When we believe in the truth about mothers and motherhood, we can rend the veil of the world's perceptions of motherhood and see ourselves with spiritual eyes.

As a mother immersed in the lives of my children, I find a variety of reminders that help me see through spiritual eyes. For example, my two-year-old daughter Bethany has a passion for Winnie the Pooh. At the beginning of one of Winnie the Pooh's adventures, Christopher Robin tells Pooh that, "You are smarter than you think. You are stronger than you seem. And you are braver than you believe."

I had a personal struggle not long ago, and I adopted this as my motto. When I felt doubt and discouragement, I would say to myself, "You're smarter than you think. You're stronger than you seem. You're braver than you believe." With this reminder, I would then take a deep breath and press forward.

Mothers should surround themselves with these messages in order to combat the adversary's lies. And just as we reinforce these ideas for our children with characters that they relate to, Our Heavenly Father does the same for us through His prophets and apostles. Here's just a sampling, First, from Elder Neal A. Maxwell: "Now, my beloved sisters, I have one reservation in speaking with you. You are already so conscientious and my desire is to lift you up, not to weigh you down. Please, remember, therefore, that as I speak, preceding any exhortation is admiration! You are likely much better than you realize."[7]

Again, from Elder Baxter:

> The Savior invites improvement to encourage us in reaching our potential. The adversary deploys derision to discourage us with feelings of worthlessness. Satan, "seeketh that all men might be miserable like unto himself" (2 Nephi 2:27). He uses the circumstances of life to drag us down so that we think less of ourselves than we should. He would have us look at how far we have yet to travel and the challenges en route, in the desire that we might give up in a state of discouragement and hopelessness.... What a difference it would make if instead we took account of our strengths, raised our eyes off the ground, and gave ourselves credit for how far we have already come and how much we have already achieved.[8]

And, finally, from President Ezra Taft Benson: "To press on in noble endeavors, even while surrounded by a cloud of depression, will eventually bring you out into the sunshine."[9]

I had a Relief Society President who counseled us, as sisters in the ward, to recognize our strengths and take account of our talents. The phrase she used to encourage this was "counsel your selves with truth."

I shared with you in the last chapter that after my second child was born, I experienced a severe case of post partum depression. When I was pregnant with my sixth child, I had this same type of depression during my pregnancy. I was interested to hear a report just a few months ago where this type of depression was just beginning to be recognized. But the way I got through this challenge in my life was to "counsel myself with truth."

The depression from my changing hormones caused me to feel discouraged at best, worthless at most. But I was able to overcome these feelings by looking into the mirror each day and telling myself that I was a daughter of God, that He loved me, that He trusted me, and that these feelings were only temporary and would pass. I would tell myself that even though it didn't feel like it, the Spirit was with me, comforting me and strengthening me. "Believe!" I would admonish my reflection in the mirror. "Believe!"

Standing there, looking at myself with spiritual eyes, I was able to, as President Benson said, "press on in my noble endeavors" of motherhood until I was at last brought "out into the sunshine."

And so it is with all mothers. I admonish you to believe! Look at yourselves with spiritual eyes and you will see beloved daughters of God called to a work of utmost importance and given the capacities and abilities necessary to accomplish that work.

R = Real & Attainable

During the October 2005 General Conference, Sister Susan W. Tanner spoke very powerfully about "real and attainable" body image. Now, I happen to believe that what happens to our physical bodies as we create, nurture, and care for children is part of the Normal Chaos of Motherhood.

After giving birth to five babies in seven-and-a-half years, my body was far from the physical ideal of the day. During that time, I had a sibling who chided me about this. I looked at him and said, "You show me the weight chart averages for women with five children, including a newborn baby. Show me the weight chart for women whose children have had half as many ear infections as mine. Show me the weight chart for women who absolutely need to eat M&Ms for comfort and consolation due to stress and fatigue. You show me that weight chart and then I'll start to worry about where I place on it!"

Having had these experiences and others, it was a pleasure to hear Sister Tanner teach us the truth about our bodies. As we proceed, we will see these truths apply to other areas of the Normal Chaos of Motherhood as well. From Sister Tanner:

> Happiness comes from accepting the bodies we have been given as divine gifts and enhancing our natural attributes, not from remaking our bodies after the image of the world. The Lord wants us to be made over—but in His image, not in the image of the world, by receiving His image in our countenances (see Alma 5:14, 19). . . . President Hinckley spoke of this very kind of beauty that comes as we learn to respect body, mind, and spirit. He said, "Of all the creations of the Almighty, there is none more beautiful, none more inspiring than a lovely daughter of God who walks in virtue with an understanding of why she should do so, who honors and respects her body as a thing sacred and divine, who cultivates her mind and constantly enlarges the horizon of her understanding, who nurtures her spirit with everlasting truth" ("Our Responsibility to Our Young Women," *Ensign*, Sept. 1988, 11). Oh how I pray that all . . . women will seek the beauty praised by the prophet—beauty of body, mind, and spirit.[10]

Prior to Sister Tanner's talk at general conference, I was blessed with another experience that taught me the same principles of body image. My husband was asked to speak at an LDS historical conference in Vermont. I took the opportunity to go with him accompanied by my seventh and still nursing baby daughter, Bethany. The highlight of the trip for me was visiting Joseph Smith's birth place. As I stepped out of the bus, the Spirit there was so strong and so palpable that I knew I was standing on sacred ground. Those attending the historical conference were afforded the opportunity to attend sacrament meeting at a chapel located on the grounds of Joseph Smith's birthplace. As I sat in sacrament meeting with my baby in my arms, my mind was filled with the powerful impression that it was not my outward appearance that I should focus on but my inward beauty—that it was the light of Christ I should be concerned about acquiring in my countenance rather than the false light of the world. These impressions surprised me. As I mentioned, my seventh baby was with me, I was still nursing her, and I had learned not to be too concerned about my body image, so while the impressions were powerful, I honestly wondered why I was receiving them.

What followed in the next year that helped me to understand and appreciate these impressions was a blessing that most women would not look at as any type of burden. But this blessing did bring with it its own share of struggles. Over the next year, almost effortlessly (with the exception of taking up running), I lost fifty pounds. Now I trust that many of you are saying in your minds, "Oh, boo hoo for you!" But believe me, it was a battle. It was a battle to remember the impressions that were so powerful in Vermont. It was a battle, as I was purchasing new clothes, to keep my mind focused on the light of Christ and away from the false but bright and blaring light of the world. It was a battle, but with the impressions from Vermont fresh in my mind, with the counsel from Sister Tanner's powerful talk, and with the help of my Savior, I was able to win that battle. I was able to keep at bay the mocking voices and pointing fingers of those in the great and spacious building, and instead, focus on the light of Christ and how I could more fully reflect Him.

Elder Jeffrey R. Holland also gave a talk in the October 2005 general conference about body image. His comments illustrate to some measure the battle I was fighting. He taught:

> Frankly, the world has been brutal to you in [regards to body image]. You are bombarded in movies, television, fashion magazines, and advertisements with the message that looks are everything! The pitch is, "If your looks are good enough, your life will be glamorous and you will be happy and popular." . . . At some point the problem becomes what the Book of Mormon called "vain imaginations." And in popular society both vanity and imagination run wild. One would truly need a great and spacious makeup kit to compete with the beauty as portrayed in media all around us. Yet at the end of the day there would still be those "in the attitude of mocking and pointing their fingers" as Lehi saw, because however much one tries in the world of glamour and fashion, it will never be glamorous enough.[11]

The key word when applying these principles taught about our physical bodies to other areas of the Normal Chaos of Motherhood is "vain imaginations." In our last chapter, Jonah referred to them as lying vanities. In short, they are our imperfect perceptions of perfection.

Take our homes for example. Let's look at the normal chaos there. I was recently at an enrichment meeting where I fell into conversation with one of the members of the Relief Society presidency. I was startled when she revealed to me that she had spoken with more than one sister in the ward who was concerned about the way they were running their homes. Each of these sisters had lamented in some way, "I just can't do it like Katie." After the initial shock of this news, I threw my head back and laughed. These women have no idea how I run my home. They do not know how clean my home is from one moment to the next. They do not know if my closets are organized or if my children's rooms are neat and tidy. What these women have conjectured in their minds with regards to my home are "vain imaginations." After I had my good laugh, I granted permission to that particular member of the Relief Society presidency to snuff out any insecurities these women were feeling by letting them know that my home is just as normal and chaotic as any other.

Just to give you an idea of the normal chaos of my home, you should know that my children do most of the cleaning. At this writing, I do not even remember the last time I turned on the vacuum cleaner. Having said that, know that my children are just as normal as other children, and they clean like other children, too. While I attempt to teach them to improve their work, I also accept their imperfect offerings just as Christ accepts my imperfect offerings. Thus, the level of cleanliness in my home is always real, and it is always attainable as opposed to "vain imaginations," which are never attainable.

There are times when I fall into "vain imaginations" myself. Once, during an unusually busy time of life, our home began to look like a tornado had blown through it. I decided that I wanted it to look perfect without any effort. I imagined how nice it would look if the Merry Maids were to come in and clean it. I even went so far as to get the telephone book down and look up their number in the yellow pages. But in the end, I rallied my troops, and together, we cleaned up our home. The bathrooms looked like boys had cleaned them. The windows were as clean as an eight-year-old could get them. I recall losing my temper at one point, but all of this afforded opportunities to teach and to learn, to repent and forgive, and ultimately, the final result was a more perfect perception of perfection than the one I had before.

Through this experience and many others like it, I can cast off my vain imaginations and embrace the truth found in the gospel. I learn that vain imaginations are never attainable, and ultimately, I learn that the counsel and guidance found in the gospel of Jesus Christ is always real. It is always attainable. And it is those real and attainable gospel goals that we should be seeking on our path towards perfection.

F = Forgiveness

Speaking of forgiveness, President Gordon B. Hinckley said, "I wish to speak today of forgiveness. I think it may be the greatest virtue on earth, and certainly the most needed. There is so much of meanness and abuse, of intolerance and hatred. There is so great a need for repentance and forgiveness. It is the great principle emphasized in all of scripture, both ancient and modern."[12]

For President Hinckley to declare as the prophet that forgiveness may be the greatest virtue on earth, makes it clear that a conversation about perfection would not be complete without commenting on forgiveness. President Hinckley also taught that forgiveness "with love and tolerance accomplishes miracles that can happen in no other way."[13]

As a mother, I am always in need of miracles in my life and in the life of my children. And if forgiveness is a crucial key to obtaining those miracles, I want to have that quality in my life. There is so much that we could look at in a section on forgiveness, but for the purposes of this chapter, I would like to focus on forgiving the one person in our lives that we tend to be the hardest on. I would like to focus on forgiving ourselves as mothers for the mistakes and missteps we've made in our lives that can sometimes seem to have such a lasting effect on our children.

There is no greater grief for a parent than to watch a son or daughter make mistakes that bring sorrow and setbacks into their lives. And as we watch our children struggle, for mothers at least, there seems to be no emotion more apparent than guilt. But consider these words from Elder Richard G. Scott:

> If you are free from serious sin yourself, don't suffer needlessly the

consequences of another's sins. As a wife, husband, or loved one, you can feel compassion for one who is in the gall of bitterness from sin. Yet you should not take upon yourself a feeling of responsibility for those acts. When you have done what is reasonable to help one you love, lay the burden at the feet of the Savior. He has invited you to do that so that you can be free from pointless worry and depression. As you so act, not only will you find peace but will [also] demonstrate your faith in the power of the Savior to lift the burden of sin from a loved one through his repentance and obedience.[14]

Read the words Elder Scott uses to describe the burdens you carry if you do not forgive yourself: worry, depression, bitterness, and suffering. Now consider the words he uses as you release yourself from the responsibility of the choices of others: peace, faith, and power. Which set of words will indicate that the miraculous power of Jesus Christ is at work in your life?

Here are just a few more descriptors used to illustrate the miraculous power that comes into your life as you forgive yourself and others: Forgiveness allows us to "rise to a higher level of self-esteem and well-being."[15] Forgiveness helps us to become "less angry, more hopeful, less depressed, less anxious, and less stressed."[16] And "forgiveness . . . is a liberating gift people can give to themselves."[17]

Dr. Sidney Simon, a recognized authority of values realization, sums up the power of forgiveness with this definition: "Forgiveness is freeing up and putting to better use the energy once consumed by holding grudges, harboring resentments, and nursing unhealed wounds. It is rediscovering the strengths we always had and relocating our limitless capacity to understand and accept other people and ourselves."[18]

As a mother, I need all of this positive potential energy to perform my everyday tasks not to say anything of the burdens of parenthood that can become too heavy to carry. And I also need that positive energy to cast those burdens upon my Savior. Because, ultimately, it is His Atoning sacrifice that makes any miracles that come into my family's life possible. As President Hinckley taught,

> The great Atonement was the supreme act of forgiveness. The magnitude of that Atonement is beyond our ability to completely understand. I know only that it happened, and that it was for me and for

you. The suffering was so great, the agony so intense, that none of us can comprehend it when the Savior offered Himself as a ransom for the sins of all mankind.

It is through Him that we gain forgiveness. It is through Him that there comes the certain promise that all mankind will be granted the blessings of salvation, with resurrection from the dead. It is through Him and His great overarching sacrifice that we are offered the opportunity through obedience of exaltation and eternal life.[19]

As we consider that humbling knowledge and contemplate the role forgiveness has in our model of perfection, let us heed the following invitation from Elder Scott: "If you have felt impressions to be free of burdens caused by yourself or others, those promptings are an invitation from the Redeemer. Act upon them now. He loves you. He gave His life that you may be free of needless burdens. He will help you do it. I know that He has the power to heal you. Begin now."[20]

E = Empathy

For the first fourteen years that my husband and I were married, we had the opportunity to attend church in some of the oldest church buildings in Utah Valley. In fact, the church building we attended when we were newly weds was called the Pioneer Chapel. With each consecutive move we made, we were amused to learn that the church we would be attending was indeed the oldest one in the area. In order to accommodate growth, each of these buildings had been added on to in peculiar ways. The most peculiar of any of the buildings we attended was designed in such a way that the only way to get from one side of the church to the other was either to go up a long flight of stairs and over the top of the chapel or to go through the gym that also served as an overflow to the chapel. I share this with you because this church is the setting for a parable I wrote depicting true circumstances in my life. To begin this section on empathy, I would like to share that parable with you. It is called "The Parable of the Door Guards."

> Now in the city of Provo, there stood a meetinghouse of ancient design. And in this meetinghouse three wards met to worship on the Sabbath Day. And as was common in those times, the meeting schedules of the wards overlapped insomuch that the ward with the late schedule need not attend meetings far into the night.

But Behold, because of the antiquity of the building, specific problems became apparent. Principally, the only places for the members to gather at the end of meetings were in two small foyers on either side of the chapel. And because the only access between these foyers was the chapel itself or the chapel's overflow, there was some commotion caused as the members attending earlier meetings went home and the members attending later meetings continued in the chapel.

Now the twelfth ward, being particularly paranoid of the lack of peace, posted door guards round about the chapel. And the duty of the door guards was to direct members of earlier meetings either up a long flight of stairs and over the top of the chapel or outside and around the chapel thus maintaining the desired degree of tranquility.

And it came to pass that attending the earlier meetings was a woman who was heavy with child. She, likewise, had been blessed with two small boys as well as the calling of primary president in her ward, the thirteenth ward.

Now on a certain Sunday, this woman, who was nearing the time when she would deliver, presented sharing time to the children of the Junior Primary. This meant that besides her belly and two small boys, she had a bag of props to bear as well.

As the thirteenth ward came to a close, the woman went with her bag, belly, and boys to meet her husband in order for him to relieve her of some of her burdens. But lo and behold as she neared the chapel she realized that the twelfth ward was in meetings, and she knew that she would not be allowed to pass over to the other side.

The woman saith to herself, "Wo, wo is me. For my strength has left me, and I cannot ascend the stairs that would allow me to cross unnoticed. Nor can I go outside to go around for my wild three-year-old would surely flee from my hands." And as she stood thinking, the woman determined to bend down and pick up her boy who had not yet reached the age of two, take her wild three-year-old by the hand and as quietly as possible make her way through the gym and across the back of the twelfth ward's meeting.

But alas, she was seen by the twelfth ward door guard, and he followed her to the other side of the chapel where the woman did find her husband waiting for her. But before she could even relieve herself of her burdens, she was seized upon by the door guard who severely chastised her for disturbing the meeting and excessively admonished her never to do it again.

Thus, the woman was left standing alone with her burdens and only a bitter feeling in her breast for companionship. And for the remainder of that Sabbath days as well as for many days afterwards, the woman's resentment towards the door guard grew for she truly felt that she had been wronged by him and that her needs had been ignored.

And time passed, and the thirteenth ward moved to the late schedule while the twelfth ward moved to the early schedule. And the woman, who had since born her third boy and was again heavy with child, found contentment in considering that the thirteenth ward had no guards posted about the chapel. Rather, the doors were left open for all to enter. Yet, peace was present and tranquility in attendance.

And lo and behold, time again passed, and the thirteenth ward moved to the early schedule while the twelfth ward moved to the late schedule, and with the changing of schedules came also the changing of the guards, and the door guards appeared again.

And the woman, now with three boys following behind her and one small baby girl in her arms, needed again to cross to the other side of the church to meet her husband. And as she made her way with her boys and her babe, she neared the chapel only to realize that the twelfth ward was in meetings.

But there stood at the door a certain door guard who noticed the woman's burdens and motioned for her to come to him. And he saith unto her, "Our meeting is nearing its end, and your arms are full. Come, and go quietly this way." And he opened the door for her and let her enter.

And the woman took those possessions that were most precious to her and crossed over to the other side. And her heart was full of gratitude and her spirit bursting with generosity. And as the woman left the meeting house that Sabbath day accompanied by these feelings of peace and joy, she beheld another ward member heavily burdened with boxes of books. And though her arms were full, she bid her oldest boy, who was now six, to hold open the door for him and let him enter.

For who amongst you having received Christlike kindness is not filled with the same charity for another? For if your Savior doth labor to serve you, "then ought not ye to labor to serve one another?" (Mosiah 2:18).

As this parable illustrates, empathy helps propel others toward correct principles and decisions. The second door guard's influence in my life was simple yet profound. He noticed and acknowledged my burdens. He cared for me and lightened my burdens by offering an easier way to get to my husband, and by doing all of this, he helped me to feel more able to turn to others and help them.

In Virginia Pearce's book, *A Heart Like His,* she relates a similar experience. She recalls that she was in her early thirties and expecting her sixth child. One day, she needed to call her friend, Phyllis, who was twenty years her senior, about some Relief Society business. Virginia relates the experience this way:

> I was about to hang up . . . when [Phyllis] asked, "Virginia, are you all right?"
>
> "What do you mean?" I said.
>
> "You just sound tired," she said with a kindness that wrapped around me like a mother's arms.
>
> "Oh," I said, talking through the tears that were suddenly choking my words. "I'm such a mess," I snuffled as I tried to explain how overwhelmed I felt.
>
> She listened for a minute and then rescued me so I could keep crying for a few minutes. "Why don't you and Jim take a couple of days off and go up to our cabin? That would give you a rest."
>
> Finally, I could talk again. "Oh, Phyllis. Thanks so much, but I don't think it'd work. It's not getting away I need. I just need to be in my house without so many people. I'm so behind. If I got away it would just be worse when I got back." Snuffle, snuffle. "But don't worry. I'll be okay. And thanks, Phyllis."
>
> "Okay, but you know that the offers good anytime."[21]

Through this experience, Phyllis was able to offer genuine empathy to Virginia. Of this empathy, Virginia writes:

> Phyllis's ability to hear my fatigue, and to care for and support me, was genuine and spontaneous. Even though she offered her cabin, it wasn't what I needed. She gave me the thing I needed—just an expression of concern, a moment of comfort, a word of encouragement . . . all others usually need from me, and all I usually need from others—and even from the Lord—is simply to be held and encircled with love while I cry a little. Then I can hang up the phone, blow my nose, and go back to work.[22]

We are all instructed that "to come into the fold of God, and to be called his people, [we must be willing to] bear one another's burdens that they may be light; yea and [be] willing to mourn with those that mourn; yea, and comfort those that stand in need of comfort" (Mosiah 18:8–9). As we do this and show one other genuine empathy, we will be able to lift and encourage one another, motivate and inspire one another, nurture and nourish one another, and ultimately change and be changed as we all progress toward that distant end marked by the loving embrace of our Heavenly Father.

C = Christ

Elder Holland tells mothers, "yours is the work of salvation, and therefore you will be magnified, compensated, made more than you are and better than you have ever been."[23] And the power magnifying us and making us better than we are is Christ. It is Christ who gives us the ability to accomplish the things we do—normal chaos and all. So the "C" in our more perfect perception of perfection is Christ.

I have shared the following journal entry many times both in speaking and writing. But it is one worth repeating because it is through this experience that I came to understand just how imperative Christ is on my journey towards perfection.

January 15, 2003

Eczema. A word I barely knew the meaning of until now, but now I know more about it then I ever wanted to know. It has been disturbing and frustrating to watch the soft silkiness of my new baby's skin be invaded by patches of red, rough, pussy sores. And it has been frightening and humbling to learn that I couldn't do anything to stop it. I read everything I could get my hands on about this skin condition. I tried "this" suggestion. I applied "that" remedy, but nothing worked. The eczema spread and worsened until I had no choice but to call the doctor.

I didn't want to call the doctor. I didn't want to take my baby in looking the way he did with sick, infected, itchy skin overpowering his bright eyes and beautiful smile. I was afraid the doctor would think I was a terrible mother. I was afraid he would gasp and exclaim, "What have you done to this baby?"

But my fears were unfounded. The doctor listened carefully to my explanation of the development of my baby's condition. He nodded and acknowledged my efforts as I discussed the things I'd already tried on my own. Then he examined my baby thoroughly, sat back on his stool, and said decisively, "You've been doing all the right things. You keep doing what you're doing and I'll help with the rest."

I felt such a sense of relief—relief and release. I had cast this burden of my baby's eczema on my doctor, and he had willingly and cheerfully taken it up for me. After following his directions for only a day, my baby's eczema improved dramatically. His itching eased so much that he was able to lay down and take the first good nap he'd had in weeks.

As I sat next to his crib, relishing the peace we were both experiencing, I reflected on my talk with the doctor. His words came back to me, "You've been doing all the right things. You keep doing what you're doing, and I'll help with the rest." These words had wiped away all my feelings of fear and doubt and had replaced them with joy and relief. I realized that it would not only be helpful but necessary to allow others to help me care for my baby, and this understanding that I was not alone in his upbringing deepened my sense of relief.

And then the words came into my mind once more, "You're doing all the right things. You keep doing what you're doing, and I'll help with the rest." Only this time, they were not the words of my doctor. They were the words of my Savior, inviting me to put away my fears and doubts and cast all my burdens upon Him. The words assured me that I could feel the same joy and relief that I felt with my baby's eczema with all my worries and troubles. They filled me with comfort as I knew that my Savior would be with me as I raised my baby. All I need do is to cast away my fear and pride and ask for His help. And just as the medication will turn the rough, red, scaly skin of my baby back to smooth and soft and silky white, the power of the Atonement will magnify my efforts and smooth over my imperfections.

We could almost end right here. The only way back to our Heavenly Father is to be perfected in Christ. He is our Advocate and Mediator. He knows and loves us. He understands our burdens and struggles. Through the power of the Atonement, we are made clean, just as my baby's eczema was made clean by the prescribed medication. But the advantage I had with the eczema medication was its immediacy. Putting our faith in Christ's healing and cleansing power is not always immediate. So we need to go to the final letter "T," which stands for time and trust.

T = Time & Trust

Our Heavenly Father is aware of us and knows our needs. He is working in our behalf to answer our prayers and help us with our perplexing problems. It is essential for our model of perfection that we trust Him and wait upon His timing. The following story illustrates this principle:

> In 1989 there was a terrible earthquake in Armenia that killed over 30,000 people in four minutes. A distraught father went in frantic search of his son. He reached his son's school only to find it reduced to a pile of rubble. But he was driven by his promise to his son, "No matter what, I'll always be there for you!" He visualized the corner where his son's classroom would be, rushed there, and started to dig through the debris, brick by brick.
>
> Others came on the scene—the fire chief, then the police—warning him of fires and explosions, and urging him to leave the search to the emergency crews. But he tenaciously carried on digging. Night came and went, and then, in the 38th hour of digging, he thought he heard his son's voice, "Armand!" he called out. Then he heard, "Dad!?! It's me, Dad! I told the other kids not to worry. I told 'em that if you were alive, you'd save me and when you saved me, they'd be saved. . . . There are 14 of us left out of 33 . . . When the building collapsed, it made a wedge, like a triangle, and it saved us."
>
> "Come on out, boy!"
>
> "No, Dad! Let the other kids out first, 'cause I know you'll get me! No matter what, I know you'll be there for me!"[24]

Like the father in this story, Heavenly Father has promised, "No matter what, I'll always be there for you!" He is tenaciously going about the business of ordering our lives so we can return to Him if, like the son in this story, we are faithful and confident in His efforts on our behalf. Even when we can't see the progress, even when we are unaware of the "digging" that is going on above us, we need to know for ourselves and encourage those around us, especially our children, that Heavenly Father is working on our behalf, and as we do our part, we will indeed be saved.

As I've already mentioned in this book, one of my favorite hymns is "Be Still, My Soul" because it is a powerful reminder of this principle:

Be still my soul: The Lord is on thy side;

> With patience bear thy cross of grief or pain.
> Leave to thy God to order and provide;
> In every change he faithful will remain.
> Be still, my soul: They best, thy Heavenly Friend
> Thru thorny ways leads to a joyful end.
>
> Be still, my soul: Thy God doth undertake
> To guide the future as he has the past.
> Thy hope, thy confidence let nothing shake;
> All now mysterious shall be bright at last.
> Be still, my soul: The waves and winds still know
> His voice who ruled them while he dwelt below.
>
> Be still, my soul: the hour is hast'ning on
> When we shall be forever with the Lord,
> When disappointment, grief, and fear are gone,
> Sorrow forgot, love's purest joys restored.
> Be still my soul: When change and tears are past,
> All safe and blessed we shall meet at last.[25]

This hymn highlights beautifully the attributes and blessings that come into our lives as we exercise trust in our Heavenly Father: patience, faith, joy, hope, confidence, light, obedience, love, safety, and blessedness! With these attributes that flow into our lives because of trusting our Heavenly Father, we can be like the little boy in the earthquake story who comforted those around him by exclaiming that his dad would come—that his dad would save him—and when his dad saved him, he would save them, too!

Conclusion

As we've tried to grasp onto a more perfect model of perfection in this chapter, we've learned that progress and striving to reach a distant end needs to be the focus of our journey. We've discussed the importance of seeing ourselves with spiritual eyes in order to believe in ourselves and our capacity to perform the tasks of motherhood. We've concluded that we must set our sights on real and attainable goals and let go of the vain imaginations of the world. We've learned about the importance of forgiveness, especially forgiving ourselves. We've come to understand the power of empathy and the unity it can bring into our lives and the lives of others as we progress along the path together. We've learned that the real power in any model of perfection is Christ and His Atonement, and we've seen that time and trust are essential in allowing Heavenly Father to work miracles in our lives and in the lives of our children. And through the stories, examples, quotes, and scriptures I've shared, I hope you've come to embrace your sometimes chaotic life as normal. Harkening back to the other unlikely truths I've highlighted in this book, I hope the stories, examples, quotes, and scriptures I've shared also help you to see that the monotony of motherhood is sweet, that the denials of motherhood are ultimately indulgences, and that pushing through the exhaustion inherent in motherhood brings a powerful exhilaration full of purpose and direction. Motherhood is a marvelous work that when performed in partnership with God brings miracles into our own individual lives and into our family's lives. Elder Holland acknowledges this with these words to mothers:

> You are doing God's work. You are doing it wonderfully well. He is blessing you and He will bless you, even—no, especially—when your days and your nights may be the most challenging. Like the woman who anonymously, meekly, perhaps even with hesitation and some embarrassment, fought her way through the crowd just to touch the hem of the Master's garment, so Christ will say to the women who worry and wonder and sometimes weep over their responsibility as mother's "Daughter, be of good comfort; thy faith hath made thee whole" (Matt. 9:22). And it will make your children whole as well.[26]

Let us, like the woman who touched the hem of Christ's garment, fight through our own crowded thoughts of uncertainty to reach out to Him. Let us push pass the attitudes of the world and press forward with faith in Christ. Let us strive to be like Christ in our service and sacrifice for our children. As we do this, we will progress along the path of perfection until we meet our distant goal of sharing the eternities with those we love and cherish most.

Notes

1. Jeffrey R. Holland, "Because She is a Mother," *Ensign*, May 1997, 35–36.
2. Ibid.
3. Russell M. Nelson, "Perfection Pending," *Ensign*, Nov. 1995, 86.
4. Ibid.
5. Ezra Taft Benson, "Do Not Despair," *Ensign*, Nov. 1974, 65.
6. David S. Baxter, "Overcoming Feelings of Inadequacy," *Ensign*, Aug. 2007, 10.
7. Neal A. Maxwell, *The Precious Promise* (Salt Lake City: Deseret Book, 2003), 1.
8. Baxter, "Overcoming Feelings of Inadequacy," 11–13.
9. Benson, "Do Not Despair," 67.
10. Susan W. Tanner, "The Sanctity of the Body," *Ensign*, Nov. 2005, 14–15.
11. Jeffrey R. Holland, "To Young Women," *Ensign*, Nov. 2005, 29–30.
12. Gordon B. Hinckley, "Forgiveness," *Ensign*, Nov. 2005, 81–84.
13. Ibid.
14. Richard G. Scott, "To Be Free of Heavy Burdens," *Ensign*, Nov. 2002, 86–88.
15. President James E. Faust, "The Healing Power of Forgiveness," *Ensign*, May 2007, 67–69.
16. Fred Luskin, in Carrie A. Moore, "Learning to Forgive," *Deseret Morning News*, Oct. 7, 2006, E1.
17. Jay Evensen, "Forgiveness is Powerful but Complex," *Deseret Morning News*, Feb. 4, 2007, G1.
18. Sidney Simon with Suzanne Simon, *Forgiveness: How to Make Peace with Your Past and Get on with Your Life* (New York: Warner Books, 1990), 19.
19. Hinckley, "Forgiveness," 81–84.
20. Richard G. Scott, "To Be Free From Heavy Burdens," *Ensign*, Nov. 2002, 86–88.
21. Virginia Pearce, *A Heart Like His* (Salt Lake City: Deseret Book, 2006), 55–58.
22. Ibid.
23. Holland, "Because She is a Mother," 35–36.
24. Mark V. Hansen, "Are You Going to Help Me?" *Chicken Soup for the Soul* (Deerfield Beach, FL: Health Communications, Inc., 2001 1993), 273–74.
25. "Be Still, My Soul," *Hymns of The Church of Jesus Christ of Latter-day Saints* (Salt Lake City: The Church of Jesus Christ of Latter-day Saints, 1985), no. 124.
26. Holland, "Because She is a Mother," 35–36.

About the Author

Katie Van Dyke is the mother of seven very active children. The whirlwind caused by these five boys and two girls exceeds even the gale-force winds that blow year round in her home town of Pocatello, Idaho. Fortunately, her husband Blair explains, that calming the "wind-storms" of life is one of Katie's great talents.

Katie holds a masters degree from Brigham Young University and is the co-author of *Stop Struggling, Start Teaching* and *Stop Struggling, Start Parenting*. Even so, she finds it interesting how unimpressed her children are with such accomplishments compared with her ability to recite *How the Grinch Stole Christmas* entirely from memory on cold winter nights when they are tucked into bed with no intention of ever going to sleep!

Among other callings in the Church, Katie has served as a counselor in the Relief Society presidency, gospel doctrine teacher, and primary president. However, if she had to choose a favorite calling it would be her time spent as the ward nursery leader. There she adopted scores of children who once a week seemed to become her own.

From all this it is safe to conclude that Katie Van Dyke loves her children, the children of the Church, and calming the gale-force winds that usually accompany them. She finds this immensely rewarding because the calmness and depth of spirit that also accompanies these energetic young souls is an invigorating influence worth savoring again and again.